The
Healing
Power of
Hormones

For my children, so that the world may be
filled with love and light like you two.

The Healing Power of Hormones

Harness dopamine,
oxytocin and serotonin
to unlock your best life

Dr Emilia Vuorisalmi

Vermilion
LONDON

1

Vermilion, an imprint of Ebury Publishing
One Embassy Gardens, 8 Viaduct Gardens,
Nine Elms, London SW11 7BW

Vermilion is part of the Penguin Random House group of companies
whose addresses can be found at global.penguinrandomhouse.com

First published by Vermilion in 2025

www.penguin.co.uk

A CIP catalogue record for this book is available from the British Library

ISBN 9781785045257

Typeset in 11.6/15.8pt Calluna by Jouve (UK), Milton Keynes
Printed and bound in Great Britain by Clays Ltd, Elcograf S.p.A.

The authorised representative in the EEA is Penguin Random House Ireland,
Morrison Chambers, 32 Nassau Street, Dublin D02 YH68

Contents

Introduction

In my home country of Finland I am known as the 'love doctor'. My mission started from my deep need to understand my own addictive behaviours and find my way back to health and balance. Shortly before I hit rock bottom, I had felt alive with every cell in my body, taking steps towards my dreams. I felt free, driving down Sunset Boulevard in LA with my windows down and the wind blowing on my face. I was going in the right direction, fulfilled and at ease.

But life's subsequent turns – getting divorced, moving back to Finland and my heart breaking in a short yet intense relationship – left me bereft and feeling out of place. I felt heavy, like my wings had been clipped before I really got the chance to fly. I returned to my native Helsinki and had to start again.

My life turned grey. Sleep evaded me. I looked from my small office window as the slush of November covered all of Helsinki under a heavy blanket. Where I once felt like I had followed my own path and lived a life where I truly felt inspired, suddenly I was drifting aimlessly, as if I had lost both my satnav and my anchor. Losing my direction turned me into a restless being.

Alongside my emotional crisis, a significant breakup left me heartbroken and screaming (literally) on the floor from the pain. This sensation stripped me of all joy. I could barely move, and successive doctors couldn't find a reason behind my constant, agonising pain. My concentration was gone and my brain was so foggy that I forgot how to get back home from the grocery store, yet I was told that there was nothing wrong with me. It was as if losing what I then thought to be the love of my life had left my body and soul utterly broken. I wanted to feel like myself again. I sought to regain my bounce the only way I knew how – through finding love again.

I fell in love with falling in love. To be honest with you, I was a master of it. I became a love addict, always searching for a new man to merge my soul with. I felt energised under the influence of this drug of love – but the high never lasted. Soon I found myself needing more of everything: the sex, the touch, the dates. Love had become toxic.

Perhaps it takes falling to rock bottom before you can slowly and diligently carve your own path back to balance. My addiction to relationships made me dive deep into the science of love. I found that when dopamine, serotonin and oxytocin – the love hormones – are in balance, we can not only heal ourselves, but also find our way to a life filled with meaning, joy and adventure. And this, dear reader, is why I'm writing this book: so that you have the tools to build a life where you feel alive and to spare you from having to make all the wrong turns that I made while you find your way back to healing and health.

Love Hormones as Our Guides

You might ask, what is so special about love hormones? Besides their leading roles in romantic love, the love hormones also work as *neuromodulators*. This means that love hormones are chemicals that also manage how other hormones work. Think of your brain as a complex network, like a bustling city. In this city, the traffic (the messages *from* and *to* your brain) is constantly moving along roads (neural pathways) to deliver information from one place (neuron) to another. In a city, traffic flow isn't just controlled by the cars and roads themselves; there are traffic lights, signs and signals that tell cars when to go, stop or slow down. These are the neuromodulators.

Neuromodulators don't send messages on their own, but *influence* how messages are sent, received and processed. They can turn up the volume on specific messages (green light), turn it down (red light) or even adjust the sensitivity of the receiving station (adjusting the brightness of the traffic light, so it's easier to see). This way, neuromodulators help regulate everything, from your mood to how you learn and respond to stress. Just like how well-placed traffic signals make for a smoother, safer ride around the city, neuromodulators help ensure that your brain's messaging system works efficiently and effectively.

So, when you work on your dopamine, serotonin and oxytocin levels and learn to build a life where these powerful molecules flow sustainably, you also indirectly work with your entire hormonal system, helping your body, mind and soul to live in true balance.

Love hormones are our internal guides that take care of how our energy is dispersed. And throughout this book you'll see this means not just your physical energy, but emotional – and spiritual – too.

Let's now take a closer look at what we actually mean when we talk about *hormones* and *energy*. Hormones are chemical messengers in the endocrine system – our body's messaging system, which is made up of glands. These glands release special molecules – hormones – which act as messengers, travelling through the bloodstream to different body parts. For example, the thyroid gland releases hormones that control how your body uses energy; the pancreas releases insulin, which helps your cells use the sugar in your blood for fuel; and the adrenal glands release stress hormones that help you respond to challenges.

Imagine your body being your home. Every household has an electric switchboard that distributes energy around the home, and your hormones are like the different switches and controls that keep everything running smoothly. Think of hormones as messengers that help your body to distribute energy and take care of its energetic balance; they work together to regulate different processes and functions, whether it's for growing new cells, processing food, having sex or fighting against an infection.

When it comes to the love hormones, dopamine gives energy direction; it wants to take you towards your purpose. (*Am I listening to my true voice? Am I connected with my joy? Am I using my creativity and superpowers – my own unique gifts that will lead me in the right direction – for common good?*) Serotonin protects this energy. (*Do I feel safe and valued? Do I value myself?*) And oxytocin connects you with other people and everything else around you. (*Are you connected to your deeper self? Do you feel that you are taken care of and that you belong?*)

When you have lost your direction in life, can't find meaning in what you do and how you spend your days and stick with the familiar out of fear or a sense of duty, these are often signs that you are slowly moving away from your soul's path. This lack of alignment with your deeper self can cause subconscious stress – as if your soul is communicating with you through mental and physical symptoms.

As I look back at the lowest time of my life, it's clear that I had lost my connection to my deeper self. I wasn't following my own path but was relying on other people to fill my life with a sense of meaning and to show me my direction. Instead of feeling safety within myself I was relying on other people's touch to calm down my restless mind. And I felt so detached from everything and everyone around me that it was hard to feel that I truly *belonged* anywhere. The source of the pain that I was trying to escape from through relationships came from the fracture of my own relationship with my deeper self.

Learning how to balance your nervous system is crucial for your entire love hormone balance, as stress hormones and love hormones are built from the same building blocks. This means that if all the blocks are used to create stress hormones, there are none left for dopamine, serotonin and oxytocin production. Your autonomic nervous system is an information highway that orchestrates where energy will be used in the body, when the stress response is activated – and thus, how your love hormones function. When you go on your journey within (as we will do in this book) you will find ways to let go of past pain and trauma that often cause subconscious stress – and build a strong base for your hormonal balance.

I've spent the last decade diving into research to understand the deeper meaning and wisdom of the love hormones. Over the years, I've realised that hormonal balance can be achieved through living aligned with your deeper self and by truly following the beat of your own heart. Every time you look to other people to set your direction in life, instead of finding your own purpose, this affects your dopamine base level. Every time you say 'yes' when you know deep down you should have said 'no', you affect your serotonin levels. Each time you feel restless, alone and separate from the people around you, your oxytocin levels are affected. So, every time you listen to your deeper self and make positive changes in how you use your energy, you end up changing your love hormone balance to provide you with more positive energy, meaning, connection and joy.

In an age where many of us tread through life without ever really drawing a full breath – drained by work, afraid of our own darkness, our days slipping away in a haze – envisioning a life that feels more energising and empowering seems far-fetched and out of reach. Financial worries and fears about the future haunt our nights. We are thirsty for intimacy but feel disconnected even in our closest relationships. We are more anxious, alone and disconnected than ever – life is passing us by and we can't seem to get a grasp on it. According to the World Health Organization (WHO), rates of anxiety and depression have risen by 25 per cent since 2020. We have never been more connected globally, yet more isolated, untethered and lonely.

Alongside this emotional depletion, many of us are at times in our lives when our hormones are imbalanced. We're so used to putting ourselves last, so we have simply given up even trying to get back to equilibrium. Feeling out of kilter has become our new normal. The days roll into weeks, then into months and we live our days in a constant fog, waiting for things to become brighter.

I have been through this darkness. However, I have learned that every twist in life is a portal to something new. My journey from rock bottom to you holding this book in your hands or listening to it has taken me through toxic relationships, hormonal imbalance, debilitating physical pain and losing the direction in my life and the connection to who I truly am. This journey has also led me through healing and finding my way back to balance. I hope this book brings you hope and gives you practical steps for how you can learn your way back to your deeper self – and true health and healing.

You don't need to be in a relationship to reap the health benefits of the love hormones. When you learn their deeper meaning, you can understand what activities and behaviours can stimulate the production of them in a sustainable and healthy way. You can begin to increase your levels of these hormones when you need them and start living more in a state of love.

Throughout this book, my aim is simple: I want to help you get to know the nature of each love hormone on a deeper level so that you can interpret the wisdom they share every day. You will be able to more easily tune into the whispers of your own body and respond to its needs immediately and with the right kind of nourishment it craves. So, instead of wandering through your days feeling empty, disconnected, unmotivated and depleted, you will have the tools to invite more joy, ease and freedom into your life, and make the right choices.

How to Use This Book

The Healing Power of Hormones is your guide to harnessing the immense power of your brain and body for health, healing and true balance. When all three love hormones are in balance, you have the potential to unlock next-level experiences in life. You will find that the more aligned you are with the source of your energy and purpose, the more likely you are to step boldly into your power, have the drive to achieve your ambitions and not be crippled by the fear of failure. You will be free to make soul-enriching, spine-tingling connections that bring technicolour vibrancy to your life and have the innate confidence and trust to love deeply and live loudly. Finding this balance is an invitation to more magic in your life. You will create an upward spiral of energy, purpose and belief which enables you to manifest even your wildest dreams.

Although I have separated the hormones out so that we approach them individually, it's worth knowing that they essentially work in harmony with each other, and that certain behaviours and habits will contribute to an uplift in more than one hormone. But for the purposes of this book and being able to access tools that you can easily apply to your life, we will look at them one by one:

- **If you ever feel like you have lost your mojo and you find it hard to take action**, learning how to balance **dopamine** will help you feel more motivated and confident.
- **If you want to feel more at peace and regulate your moods**, focus on **serotonin**, the hormone that is your foundation for finding long-lasting calm and equilibrium.
- **Balancing your oxytocin will bring you back to your deeper self and create a sense of connectedness** with the world around you.

The book is structured in three parts. Part One is a deep dive into the world of **dopamine**. Dopamine is associated with drive, rewards and an overall sense of well-being and energy. I see dopamine as the hormone of direction; it can help you to get back to your soul's unique path and fill your days with purpose. In this section, you'll learn about how modern life has leaned heavily on the instant beguiling rush of dopamine, creating a dependence on 'fast', unsustainable forms of this powerful hormone, such as gaming late into the night, online shopping, addictive processed food and other drugs, both legal and not, which hit our bliss points in unhealthy ways and leave us grappling for more and more! This often creates a pattern of peaks and troughs, where the highs become less enjoyable and the lows become ever lower. Throughout Part One, you will build your understanding of how this neurotransmitter works its magic on your system and find different ways of incorporating more of the healthy, desirable sources of dopamine into your life. You will gradually learn how to replace your reliance on unhealthy dopamine spikes with more sustainable, equally uplifting forms of dopamine which will enable you to feel more joy and motivation day to day, without the crashes that often follow. With the wisdom of dopamine, you can find your way back to life where your days are filled with gladness and meaning – and where you are following your dreams.

In Part Two, we roam through the compassionate world of **serotonin**. We need this incredible neurotransmitter to ensure that we feel physically and emotionally healthy – it is a key hormone that helps us to feel safe so that we have the courage to take the leap and shine our light. When serotonin is at normal levels, you feel more focused, emotionally stable, happier and calmer. Depression and anxiety are the most common result of a reduction in serotonin, alongside sleep problems and digestive issues – a general feeling of being slightly off kilter. This part will walk you through ways you can create a more stable serotonin system by learning how to protect your energy and build a strong sense of safety from within.

Part Three is all about snuggling up in the warm, loving arms of **oxytocin**. Oxytocin, often referred to as the cuddle hormone, is the hormone of affection and touch, the key ingredient for parent–child bonding, giving us fuzzy feelings of deeply connected human relationships – but you will find that it's so much more than that. This is the neurotransmitter that facilitates human bonding, social connection and helps to regulate our emotional responses. When oxytocin is optimum, you feel connected to your partner and your close circle of friends, empathy is higher, communication is more effective, overall stress levels are reduced and well-being is heightened. On top of this, oxytocin is the hormone of connection – with both your deeper self and everything around you. In this part, you will find ways to reconnect with yourself so you can notice the good in life, feel calm and at peace again in every cell of your body and held by everything around you.

Within each of these three parts I will look at specific, proven ways of seeking a healthy balance of these hormones. All the tools are grounded in medical understanding of biology and science, tied with ancient wisdom and quantum medicine. In each chapter I will guide you through some inner work to excavate the deeper blockages or deeply rooted pain you might be experiencing right now that may prevent your love hormones from flowing freely in balance. I want to embolden you to travel further into your deepest, most intimate and private spaces guarding your spirit, and here I will offer holistic, spiritual and somatic practices, such as breathwork and meditation, that can unlock the next stage of your transformation. It is often here, in that space just outside your comfort zone, that the real truths are revealed for you to move forward and actually live the life you have dreamed of.

There are also 'Over to you' boxes throughout the book, designed to provide you with space to pause, breathe and reflect on how the themes in each chapter are resonating within you. These are opportunities to ask yourself thoughtful questions and consider what steps you might feel able to take right away. I wrote this book to enable you to deep dive into your own immense potential, as well as to be a practical guide from where you can pick up practices for your daily life. When you apply the elements that resonate most with you and your life, you are curating your own personal recipe for transformation, blossoming into the person you were meant to be.

Remember as you work your way through this book that it is unrealistic to expect that we should feel happy, content and energised *every moment* of *every day*. However, you *can* increase your chances of feeling this way more of the time, increasing your emotional resilience and overall well-being.

Why me?

I've been a private practitioner for over a decade, creating space where I can be a doctor in my own way. For too long I tried to squeeze myself into the traditional role of a medical doctor, treating only the symptoms and not having the time to truly *be* with my patients. Fighting against who you really are is a draining battle and never results in empowering outcomes. The moment I had the courage to jump out of the box and express myself and my superpowers without fear, not only did my work life change, but my whole life.

Today, I help people find true balance on different platforms. Together with a team of other like-minded holistic visionaries, we are now building a clinic that not only provides patients with a holistic model of care, but also creates a space where doctors can truly connect with their patients using a holistic approach to help them heal. I have written two bestselling books about love hormones that have been translated into multiple languages. I have had my own TV show and podcast and, through my one-to-one and online coaching, I have helped thousands of people towards better balance. I have been the team doctor and co-owner of the men's basketball team Helsinki Seagulls, and also played a lead role in a primetime Finnish romantic comedy. I try to live as I preach – doing things that bring me joy and give me energy, and living a life where I have the courage not to put myself into a box! What I've learnt is to never underestimate what you can achieve when you have the courage to follow your dreams, are connected with your true self and surround yourself with great, like-minded people.

In this book I have blended my scientific knowledge and years of practice as a doctor with my own experience of transformation and growth from despair to fully thriving. In my work my aim is to build bridges and bring old and new wisdom together. I also want to be on the frontiers, asking questions and bringing people new perspectives on life and health. I hope that you, too, will find your way to your deepest most authentic self and the magic it can bring.

I want your main take-homes from this book to be an understanding of the key elements of each hormone and the wisdom that they all carry so that you can tap into the distinct needs within your body or mind and know what you can do to help your love hormones to flow sustainably. This way, you'll finish the book with your own bespoke toolkit for living a life of meaning, creativity and deep-rooted joy – feeling happier, more energised and vibrant, every day.

May this book be a lantern in the dark, guiding you to your own path of transformation and fulfilment. I can't wait to go on this journey with you!

Please take care of yourself as you move into this journey of inner work and introspection. I am a medical doctor, but this book does not offer guidance around clinical depression, anxiety or medication for supplementing any physical or mental symptoms. If you are suffering from mood disorders, chronic anxiety, depression or pain that require deeper levels of intervention, please reach out without delay to your healthcare practitioner.

Part 1

Dopamine: The Hormone of Direction

Chapter 1

What is Dopamine?

Dopamine is the hormone of *direction* and *reward*. Dopamine motivates us to reach new hights and outdo ourselves, time after time. You can think of dopamine as the risk-taker that loves standing on the edge and exploring new possibilities. If dopamine was an investment banker, it would invest in high-risk, high reward stocks, keeping its focus on the future rewards.

Dopamine is basically behind every step we take. Healthy levels are crucial for motivation, reward, pleasure, alertness, mood, focus and a sense of positive drive and well-being. Whether that's the decision to grab a cup of coffee, pick up your phone or declutter your home, dopamine is fuelling you to take action. But dopamine has a deeper role, too: at its core, everything is energy and dopamine's deeper meaning is to give this energy direction towards your purpose in life.

When we are connected to our true purpose, we have inner peace that protects us from seeking out dopamine from unsustainable, even toxic sources. Living a life aligned with your true direction and purpose is the key to building a thriving dopamine system based on sustainable dopamine sources, and will reflect on your health even at a cellular level.

Dopamine helps drive motivation and goal-directed behaviour – it enables us to pursue rewards and take action to achieve our goals. In addition, dopamine is critical for motor control. It helps coordinate smooth, voluntary movements. Disorders like Parkinson's disease are associated with low levels of dopamine, leading to symptoms such as tremors and difficulty with movement. On the other hand, movement can be a powerful source of dopamine, making things like dance and exercise a good way to boost dopamine in our daily lives.

Dopamine also influences cognitive processes, including attention, learning and memory. When an enjoyable activity or rewarding experience occurs, dopamine is released into the brain. It binds to specific receptors on neurons, transmitting signals that produce feelings of pleasure and satisfaction. After dopamine has transmitted its signal, it is either reabsorbed by the neuron that released it (a process called reuptake) or broken down by enzymes. This helps regulate the levels of dopamine in the brain.

Dopamine is released in greatest amounts when the brain is *anticipating* a reward: imagine the waggy tail of a dog excited to go for a walk – this is the essential nature of dopamine. The flood of dopamine to the brain when experiencing pleasure (such as enjoying delicious food, playing video games or having sex) ultimately reinforces our *intrinsic reward system*. We then respond by developing unconscious patterns and habits based on this reward, ensuring that we seek more of this pleasurable activity. Our brains ultimately want to ensure our survival and are constantly seeking the best ways of making sure we behave in a way that will keep us alive. The bottom line is that human survival is evolutionarily linked to our brain seeking rewards and pleasure, therefore helping us to grow strong and find the best sources of food and environment to settle. This is part of our innate pro-gramming: the biological need for food, sex and the social interactions and community bonds which will provide safety. However, as we will learn throughout this part of the book, the world that we live in doesn't take into consideration this ancient biology weaved into our human condition. As a result, too much pleasure can soon turn into pain.

The Dark Side of Dopamine

When your dopamine levels are not balanced, you can easily lose direction. This is the road to becoming hooked on easy-access, quick-fix dopamine from unsustainable sources outside us – short-lived, instant-hit dopamine from a sub-stance or a behaviour, such as fast food, endless mindless scrolling, drugs or alcohol. Unsustainable dopamine sources create an immediate substantial elevation in dopamine levels, causing you to feel the positive effects of energy and meaning instantly, like a soothing balm. However, the effect is short-lived and soon you need more to have the same effect.

When our dopamine system is unbalanced, it can also be the source of us feeling like we have missed our calling, fearing we are not good enough and haven't fulfilled our potential – that we have lost our way. This is why building our dopamine system merely on external, short-lived dopamine sources is unsustainable for our mental, physical and spiritual well-being. We need to follow our own direction in life so that we can live with meaning; a life where we express our unique superpowers, thrive and feel fully alive.

When you don't follow your own direction in life you create a gap between you and your deeper self. This gap, a misalignment with your true self, creates a space for pain to enter. And we will do almost anything to not feel that pain in our heart. From that void, many addictive behaviours stem. Like in my case, my addiction to love.

Understanding this dark side of dopamine and identifying where the dangers lie means you can unlock the capacity to create a new blueprint for your reward system, and recognise your achievements, success and potential within a different framework. You'll come to see why, for sustainable positive drive and well-being, learning how to build a healthy dopamine system, stemming from sustainable dopamine sources, is the key to a life that truly fulfils you – and makes you feel like you are exactly where you should be.

And at the centre of this work is learning to understand how our dopamine baseline works, the nature of peak experiences and how they are at the heart of addiction.

The dopamine baseline

The term 'dopamine baseline' refers to the steady level of dopamine present in your system when you are doing nothing special. When you have a healthy dopamine baseline, you have enough dopamine circulating in your system, making you feel motivated and well.

When your dopamine baseline drops, and your dopamine levels are below the baseline, a feeling of emptiness takes over your entire being. It's as if you have no energy left and no motivation to move forward. This drop can leave you with difficulties focusing, staying attentive and processing information. You feel fatigued and low in energy, and it's hard for you to stay motivated and engaged in life. Your body can even feel stiff and in pain due to your dopamine levels crashing.

Many of us can't stand this sense of emptiness and low energy that comes from dopamine levels dropping below the baseline and we turn outside ourselves to unsustainable sources of dopamine for quick relief. Unsustainable dopamine sources include things like searching for the next date on Tinder, always planning for the next big trip abroad, working excessively or turning to food or alcohol.

With social media, we have constant access to fast digital dopamine. There is instant gratification through likes and comments, triggering dopamine release in the brain. With every tap, there is something new coming at you. The edits on the videos are often fast, creating a sense of excitement and anticipation as your attention is constantly shifting, leading to an increase in your dopamine release. Also, the unpredictability of fast-paced editing together with an unlimited flow of content can increase dopamine levels as you never know what is coming next – and there is always more.

The challenge with these unsustainable dopamine sources is that the 'high' they initially produce soon loses that effect, so you quickly need *more* in order to get the same good mood and positive drive you had before. This is the nature of dopamine – it always leaves us wanting more: more shopping, more screen time, more sex, more work.

When you start the inner work of balancing your dopamine system, building a healthy dopamine baseline and finding your way back to your deeper self, as we will do later in this part of the book, it's all about setting the direction and less about the speed. Many of us, me included, are impatient and want to have everything at once. Instead of taking the time, sitting with the discomfort of naturally getting your dopamine levels back to sufficient levels and letting insights emerge, we run in the wrong direction. Old ways do not open new doors. When you start your inner work and change your dopamine sources from unsustainable to sustainable, your best friend is patience.

As we've explored, dopamine is the hormone of direction – a power system within each of us, igniting the fire to create and fuel us with the energy and drive to move forward with our dreams. When we are going in our own direction, life feels fulfilling and light, as if we are swimming downstream. When we are not following the direction of our own soul, life can start feeling empty – and emptiness can create a space for addiction to enter.

Addiction: Our attempt to mask the pain

As I touched on in the Introduction, when I hit rock bottom, I turned to the source of what I knew had always helped me to calm myself and to take away the pain: sex and relationships. I learned to 'medicate' myself by falling in love. I would grab on to feelings of lust and physical chemistry like a lifeline. The high of that early phase of romantic love was my escape from the emptiness I was feeling.

For me, receiving the love of someone else was the biggest prize. Every time in the early phase of a relationship, I would get a familiar boost of giddy energy. I felt alive and energised and, for a while, the ripple effect was that my life had a new sense of direction. My life felt empty and boring without a man in it. My business partner even joked, 'you don't need to sign an NDA with Emilia but a NAFL – Not Allowed to Fall in Love'. The hormonal cocktail of early love healed my pain and made me feel like myself again.

But soon the high of early love turned dark. As a love addict, I had trained my dopamine system to rely heavily on peak experiences for dopamine. 'Peak experiences' are situations where a short-lived dopamine source, such as a one-night stand, getting a promotion or winning a marathon, leads to a considerable increase in dopamine circulating in our system. These peak experiences are highly pleasurable, even ecstatic, making us long for these moments in the future. You start immediately planning for the next race, or you take on a new, big project. From the viewpoint of a brain relying mostly on peak experiences for its dopamine, you always need something to strive for, a reason to push. However, after these peak experiences, we often feel empty – after the highly pleasurable feelings of the chase, the result, the prize we had been waiting for, can feel close to nothing. With my own addiction to relationships and love, I soon noticed how I started needing more of it – the texting, the dating, the sex, the touch – just for it all to have the same calming effect on me that it had before. This is the nature of dopamine; it wants more and is not picky about the 'how'.

In the long run, overloading the brain continuously with dopamine causes our dopamine receptors to become less sensitive. When our dopamine system relies on external sources, we are driven to attain more. And the more we get, the more our tolerance for dopamine grows. This means that the same level of the substance or activity no longer produces the same level of pleasure and satisfaction. As a result, the baseline drops even further, making it harder for us to sustain the previous dopamine level. We notice that to achieve the same 'high' or sense of reward, we need to increase the dose or frequency of the behaviour – we need to buy even more giant bags of candy and spend longer scrolling mindlessly through social media – to have the same neurochemical effect on us that it had before.

This can lead to the development of tolerance and, ultimately, dependence or addiction. We may start to crave the substance or activity as our brain has become 'rewired' to seek out the altered state or feeling of pleasure – this is known as *neuroadaptation*.

This neuroadaptation process can occur with a wide range of rewarding experiences, including drugs, alcohol, gambling, sex and even love. Instead of feeling fulfilled in my quest for love, I began to feel detached and not like myself. I was restless. Often the first sign of this was my screen time beginning to spin out of control, constantly checking my phone for messages from the object of my desire. Simply *being* was impossible. My attention and focus were lost, and I was unable to concentrate on – well, anything. I could no longer sit down to read a book. I didn't have the attention span to even watch a movie.

This continuous desire for more is also driving most of our Western culture and devouring our planet. We convince ourselves that we need to have a bigger house, a better car or a more extravagant everyday life. We try to consume our way to meaning and purpose. In our attempt to fill the emptiness, we overspend. But, instead of giving us the feeling of freedom and joy we so crave, continuously acquiring more can enslave us.

Maybe you recognise yourself in this description, or perhaps you have come to rely on quick dopamine sources such as sugary food, alcohol or social media to help you fill a sense of emptiness inside or give you pleasure. Fast dopamine sources easily create a negative circle, where we need more but are, as it happens, getting less of the positive drive, energy and sense of inspiration and well-being we were initially looking for. Understanding neuroadaptation is crucial not only to understand your addictive behaviours, but also to work on rebuilding your dopamine system from unsustainable, fast sources to rely more on sustainable sources.

As a love addict, I needed to lose myself in love. By losing myself, I got my sense of direction again. I got the story I was yearning for; the story of being 'the partner' gave me meaning and provided direction for dopamine to flow. As I discovered, ultimately this did not serve me well. We need to provide our own inner north star – following the coordinates of others simply veers us off the right course for us. And at the centre of this work is learning to understand how our dopamine baseline works and the nature of peak experiences.

Whatever your quick fix, relying on unsustainable dopamine sources can affect us in many ways:

- **Our cravings for instant rewards increase.** This heightened craving can drive people to engage in addictive behaviours in an attempt to satisfy the need for dopamine release. This means that we can become increasingly hungry for likes on social media or even more competitive and want to win.
- **We become less sensitive to rewards.** This means that we lose the sense of pleasure and satisfaction from activities that would usually be enjoyable to us. Normal isn't enough anymore: our hobbies and our social circles don't seem to bring the same pleasure that they used to.
- **The pain–pleasure balance shifts to the pain side.** We start masking the pain with quick dopamine sources.

- **It may be harder for us to maintain focus and make informed decisions,** and we can find ourselves procrastinating or engaging in activities that prevent us from achieving our goals.

With unsustainable dopamine sources and peak experiences, it's like surfing a massive wave in a swimming pool. The wave is high, and your every cell feels excited. However, the power of the wave also makes the water move outside the pool. It splashes all over the floor, knocking over anything that comes in its way. As a result, the pool's water is only a fraction of what it was before surfing. And we feel as empty as the swimming pool: we have used all the available dopamine in our system.

When you start craving unsustainable dopamine sources to feel a temporary sense of meaning and purpose, it can create havoc for your dopamine system. Instead of creating more fulfilment, relying on peak experiences can end up making you feel lower than ever. And to take the pain away, you go again. And a negative spiral of addiction is created.

By trying our best to escape discomfort and maximise our happiness, we are actually doing ourselves a disservice. This is because, as with everything in life, there is also a balance between pain and pleasure. Dr Anna Lembke describes this as the 'pleasure–pain balance' in her book *Dopamine Nation: Finding Balance in the Age of Indulgence*. The more the scale tips on the side of pleasure, the more pain our dopamine system needs to get back to balance. As you already learned with the dopamine baseline, the low-dopamine state can feel both physically and mentally painful to us. On top of suffering from pain in our bodies (as I did with my continuous back pain that seemingly had no evident cause) the shame, depression and despair can be a pain that reaches all the way to the soul.

We are built for seeking; we need to feel uncomfortable and work hard for meaningful things. For our ancestors, seeking food was essential for survival. Dopamine was essential for providing that drive and desire to go out and actively find food, a process which may have been dangerous, arduous and tiring, but that brought an intrinsic reward – a reward from within: a feeling of satisfaction, for performing behaviours that kept us alive.

In our modern world, at least here in the global West, the majority of us no longer need to go through the process of working through discomfort for things like food. We are not involved in the process of growing the ingredients. We don't even need to make the food we eat. We can just click a button in an app on our smartphones and a ready-to-eat meal will soon be delivered to our doorsteps. Just like that!

For our ancient dopamine system this is a challenge. Our dopamine system needs discomfort so that the pleasure–pain scale can stay in balance. In order to fill our days with positive drive and a sense of well-being and energy, our dopamine system relies on us having meaningful things in our life that we can work for.

Meaning drives dopamine. This is why working in a job that you don't feel connected with, that doesn't align with your core values, or performing tasks only for others can actually be harmful for your dopamine system. When you are connected to your dreams and following your own authentic path, you are building a healthy dopamine system that flows in balance from your daily actions.

Sometimes we can drive ourselves into addictive behaviours by having too much pleasure in life. More often than not, however, I have seen how the pain from being disconnected with our deeper selves and not following our own direction in life causes addictive behaviours. We try our best to hide or run away from the pain that comes from this deep misalignment.

When there is pain to be masked, even the healthiest of things can become addictive. We often think of the pleasure we get from a substance or a behaviour being the addictive component. However, as author Dr Anna Lembke points out, it is the pursuit of escaping the pain that characterises addiction. She insightfully outlines that sometimes the most painful thing we can do is to be alone with our thoughts and feel our feelings. Lembke writes, 'We'll do almost anything to distract ourselves from ourselves.'

Our society shapes how we view addictive behaviours. A person who runs away from emotional pain by working excessively can be viewed as an inspirational go-getter, even though the addiction to work is creating havoc in all the other areas of their life and causing both mental and physical symptoms. Even self-development can become an ongoing project where there is always more to improve, leaving us disconnected and searching for meaning from outside ourselves, wanting to fit a form instead of being true to ourselves. Or a person who is running away from the emptiness by always training for the next marathon is perceived as a dedicated, high-performing athlete, instead of a person possibly fleeing from pain by looking for a sense of purpose and always seeking another goal to strive for.

Why can love be so addictive?

In the early phase of romantic love, also called the 'honeymoon phase', you are, quite literally, high on love. You are bewitched and obsessed with the object of your desire, unable to think of anything else. You may find that sleep eludes you and you lose your appetite. You might never want to leave your bed, so intense is the sexual desire and the euphoric feeling of connection and meaning. The high dopamine levels of this stage ensure that your focus and highest goal is to be with your loved one.

While the honeymoon phase can be blissful and overwhelming, it's also intense and can strain the body and the mind, thanks to the high levels of stress hormone cortisol. Thankfully, nature has designed that within 18 months after meeting, all the intense energy has the potential to transform into a calmer and more serene state of love. This state is the attachment state. The honeymoon phase's intense longing and obsessive desire have transmuted into a firm, anchored sense of security and relaxed curiosity about the future. As a result, we feel at peace and calm. Based on nature's agenda, this stage is designed to be the neurochemical soil in which the parents will care for their young, helping them raise a family.

When a relationship evolves from the euphoric high of the honeymoon phase to the attachment stage, it can be a big change for your brain, body and mind. Imagine how the brain has been used to floating in a high-dopamine and high-cortisol state. Has it been straining for the system? Yes. Has it been exciting and high-energy? Yes. When this high-energy state begins to transform thanks to the hormonal levels of dopamine, serotonin and oxytocin changing, and stress hormone levels lowering, some of us can start feeling unease with this new, even 'boring' state.

To get the stress hormones and dopamine on its previous high-level state and to 'feel like us again' (as I did), our system can perceive this new calmer state as dangerous (you will learn more about this in Part Two), recognising it as a red flag. We might go and do something to sabotage the relationship. We may start fights so that our cortisol, adrenaline and dopamine levels rise (when we fight, our dopamine levels increase together with stress hormones to help us take action).

Sometimes the end of a relationship can shake our system. All of the great love stories, such as Jack and Rose from *Titanic*, Tony and Maria from *West Side Story* and Romeo and Juliet, show what happens when the love ends in the incredible high of the honeymoon phase: the heartache, the pain, the loss. We often think that a short fling or a summer romance should hurt less because it was quick. However, from a neurobiological perspective, this sudden change can feel like we are losing ourselves and cause withdrawal symptoms. When a relationship ends, the dopamine levels are often still elevated, making us obsessed with the target of our affection. However, the longer we are away from the person of our desires, the more complex the withdrawal symptoms can become.

Passion creates and addiction consumes

By now I hope you have learned how when we talk about dopamine and addiction it is never black and white. Are all hard-working business go-getters driven by emotional pain? No. Are all long-distance runners or extreme sport enthusiasts trying to suppress something by training hard and pushing themselves to the limit? No, this would be a drastic simplification and assumption on how someone else's dopamine system is built.

How addictive a behaviour or a substance might be is always personal. This is because it is the person who attaches the meaning to whatever they think to be the ultimate goal. For me, it was being high on love; for Dr Lembke, it was erotic novels. Dr Maté has openly discussed his addiction to classical music records and even leaving a woman in labour at the hospital to go and get a CD from the record shop. Perhaps the essence of overcoming addiction is that, when you have found balance, the choice (whether work, shopping or relationships) comes from a place of freedom – the freedom of walking your own path and no longer making your decision based on past pain.

To find a more sustainable flow of dopamine and break free of the cycle of addiction to support a healthy dopamine baseline, it's crucial to create inner sources of dopamine to fuel your days with purpose and a sense that you are moving in the right direction for your life. I call this the inner work that guides you towards your unique path of meaning. You can do this by:

- **Reconnecting with your joy:** Joy gives us energy and helps get us back on track when we are lost. In Chapter 6 I will help you remember what lights the sparkle in your soul by using your unique creativity and superpowers.
- **Having the courage to walk your own path:** It takes courage to break free from the expectations of our outer world. In Chapter 3 we will focus on how to start living a life aligned with your dreams and values – moving you towards your purpose. You'll see how every step then becomes a sustainable source of dopamine.
- **Making it happen:** In Chapter 4 we'll harness the power of neuroplasticity and explore tools that will enable you to make your dreams come true.

In the following chapters you will discover ways to naturally and slowly charge up your dopamine power, find your own direction and build a life that energises every cell in your being. You might be wondering whether there's anything you can do right in this moment to support your dopamine system. Long-lasting change comes from the inner work we are doing throughout this book. However, there are some simple things you can do to support you on this journey back to balance.

Support your inner journey

The thing is, life happens. Life is a continuous wave of highs and lows, and nothing stays stagnant – especially when we are working on rebalancing our dopamine system. These practices are great ways to support your daily dopamine levels:

Eat dopamine-boosting food

We all know how we feel when we haven't eaten food that is truly good for us. We become bloated and feel heavy and restless. Sleep doesn't recharge us and our brain is foggy. When we eat food that is nourishing for us – nutrient dense, clean and colourful food – we can see the effects surprisingly quickly. Your energy levels rise, your skin looks better and research shows that changes in your diet can also be seen in your gut microbiome the next day.

The better our hormonal and personal balance is, the easier it is for us to eat well intuitively. When we are off balance, we often need to actively pay more attention to how we support our dopamine system with our daily actions. Here are some tips on how you can support your dopamine system with nutrition.

- **Small actions that set the tone for the day**: Try to start the day with a glass of lemon water to support your dopamine system. This routine will not only rehydrate you and help to balance your hormones, but it gets the morning off to a good start.

- **Focus on foods rich in tyrosine:** This amino acid is a key element in dopamine creation. You'll find tyrosine in nuts and seeds, such as almonds and pumpkin seeds, avocados, eggs, lean meats such as chicken and turkey, and lentils and chickpeas.

- **Include sources of phenylalanine:** An amino acid that converts into tyrosine. Examples include lean meats, fish, cheese, tofu, edamame beans and seeds such as sesame. Sprinkle seeds on your yoghurt, add some cheese to your salad. You can be creative!

- **Increase vitamin B6 and folate:** These vitamins play a role in dopamine synthesis. My favourite sources are beans, spinach, broccoli, citrus fruits and bananas.

- **Load up on antioxidants:** Oxidative stress – an imbalance between harmful free radicals (which can come from things like pollution, unhealthy foods and natural metabolic processes) and protective antioxidants in the body, leading to cellular and tissue damage over time – can negatively affect dopamine. Eating plenty of antioxidant-rich foods can help protect these receptors. Eat more berries (blueberries, strawberries – frozen is fine!), leafy greens (spinach, kale), cruciferous vegetables (broccoli, cauliflower) and citrus fruits (oranges, grapefruits).

- **Healthy fats are our friends:** Olive oil, omega-3 fatty acids found in fatty fish, walnuts, chia seeds and flaxseeds are beneficial for brain health and dopamine regulation. Listen to your intuition and try different sources of healthy fats to support optimal dopamine levels.

- **Fermented foods:** Yoghurt, kefir, sauerkraut and kimchi promote a healthy gut microbiome and can potentially support balanced dopamine levels.
- **Dark chocolate:** A great source of magnesium and also helps to boost your dopamine levels. I treat myself every day to some dark chocolate (preferably minimum 70 per cent cocoa).
- **Opt for whole grains:** Brown rice, quinoa, oat and wholewheat, which provide complex carbohydrates that can help stabilise blood sugar levels and support dopamine regulation.
- **Incorporate spices and herbs:** Turmeric, ginger and black pepper may support healthy dopamine levels through their anti-inflammatory and neuroprotective properties. Herbs like basil and rosemary have been shown to have neuroprotective effects and may enhance dopamine function. Spices are also an easy way to add more colours and antioxidants to your food!
- **Pause before eating:** Nothing absorbs well when you are stressed or eating in a hurry. Before starting your meal, pause and take a few deep breaths. This can help you transition into a more mindful and focused state, which can enhance your digestion and the absorption of nutrients.
- **Remember the 80/20 rule:** When 80 per cent of your food is healthy and nutritious, 20 per cent can be almost anything.

When you start noticing how much better eating well makes you feel, the easier and natural it soon becomes to maintain a diet that nourishes your body and soul. This way, nutrition will become a strong pillar for your dopamine system, too.

Be mindful of your coffee. Caffeine is a stimulant and can cause your central nervous system to become wired, which impacts on how you regulate your dopamine. On the other hand, caffeine also protects dopaminergic neurons. Instead of drinking coffee first thing in the morning, you can try to extend the time between waking up and grabbing your first cup of joe. Our cortisol levels naturally peak in the morning, at around 8 or 9am, so drinking coffee when these levels are already high can lead to an excess of stimulation, which may impact sleep and cause jitteriness. Waiting until after 9am but before 11am, when cortisol levels start to decline, allows the coffee to have a more balanced effect. Keeping your coffee intake moderate and finding a sweet spot in the middle will take you a long way!

In the afternoon, instead of grabbing a cup of coffee and a sugary snack to give you an energy boost, try matcha or green tea paired with some dark chocolate. Matcha is rich in L-theanine, an amino acid that promotes relaxation without drowsiness. Matcha contains caffeine, but the presence of L-theanine modulates its effects. This combination provides a sustained energy boost without the jitteriness or crashes associated with coffee. If you are not ready to drop coffee, you can also blend it with matcha and hot milk (of your choice) like I do!

Dark chocolate, on the other hand, contains phenylethylamine, a compound that acts as a natural stimulant and can promote the release of dopamine in the brain. Dark chocolate also contains small amounts of caffeine and a compound called theobromine. Both of these compounds can increase alertness and improve mood, without as intense a crash as coffee.

Prioritise sleep and deep rest

Just one bad night of sleep can reduce dopamine drastically – which is partly why new parents are so susceptible to low mood. Your body recharges and replenishes during sleep. It is such a core factor that it needs to be central in your plan to optimise your dopamine health.

There is a lot of talk about sleep these days and I bet you, too, have seen lists on what you can do to improve your sleep; I sure have had my share of those lists (being also the one creating some of them). However, even I forget some of these things from time to time. Below are some of my favourite tips for a sleep routine that you can implement to support recharging sleep alongside the inner work we are going to do throughout the book:

- **Limit exposure to screens:** The blue light from your devices disrupts your sleep–wake cycle. Avoid screens – and particularly multi-screening – for at least an hour before bed. I avoid taking my phone to the bedroom and keep my sleeping space screen-free.

- **Avoid stimulants before bed:** Be mindful about caffeine. Caffeine metabolism is highly individual. For example, I am sensitive to the stimulating effects of caffeine and know not to have any coffee after 3pm because it affects my sleep. When you feel like having a cup of coffee during the day, ask yourself: *Do I really need it or would a quick walk or a breathing exercise be more beneficial?*

- **Collect all colours of light:** Sunlight is the conductor that organises the symphony of different processes in our bodies. Sunlight sets our circadian rhythm and communicates to our cells when it is time to start producing hormones, such as melatonin and serotonin, that encourage us to fall asleep. Exposing your eyes to sunlight first thing in the morning can help your body to set up its internal clock properly and support you in falling asleep in the evening. Don't forget to expose your eyes to the midday sun and the red-orange hues of the sunset – all these colours are information to your system and assist it to run in balance. Of course, always take care not to look directly at the sun.

- **Create a relaxing bedtime routine:** A soothing routine signals to your body that it's time to wind down. Slow activities such as reading a book, taking a warm bath, restorative yoga or meditation or listening to calming music can signal to your nervous system that all is good and that it's safe to relax and rest.

- **Try these supplements:** Vitamin B6, Magnesium glycinate and L-theanine can help you wind down and fall asleep.

- **Sometimes we wake up during the night and have a hard time falling back to sleep:** Using 4-7-8 breathing can help you to fall back to sleep. Inhale for 4 seconds, hold your breath for 7 seconds and exhale for 8 seconds. This seems to be a natural rhythm for us when we yawn and feel relaxed – and can work like magic!

If regular deep overnight sleep evades you, focus on deep rest. This is waking rest, such as yoga nidra (see page 160) or Non-Sleep Deep Rest (NSDR). Neuroscientist Andrew Huberman brought this powerful technique to the masses and explained how a 30-minute NSDR session can increase dopamine levels in the brain area called the striatum by an astonishing 65 per cent.

Get enough morning sunlight

Make sure that you balance your dopamine system daily by getting enough sunlight every day. Preferably morning sunlight – in the 30 minutes after waking up – and without sunglasses. Even on a cloudy day, the amount of daylight received by your retina plays a core role in dictating your dopamine production. Sixteen hours after morning sunlight exposure, the melatonin production activates. This means that exposure to morning sun helps you to fall asleep better in the evening. And as you learned before, sleep is one of the core pillars for a healthy dopamine system.

Move your body

Alongside the psychological movement towards goals that light up your soul and make your entire being feel alive, dopamine is also released by physical movement. Physical activity, whether it's aerobic exercise like running or cycling, strength training or incidental and playful movement, such as dancing, leads to the release of dopamine in the brain. Regular exercise has been shown to increase the sensitivity of dopamine receptors in the brain. This means that the dopamine that is released during exercise can have a stronger effect, leading to increased feelings of pleasure and reward from other dopamine sources, too.

Follow any type of movement that brings you joy. It can be ballroom dancing, weightlifting or jogging. Sometimes less can be more – just ten minutes of running or biking can give you a little dopamine boost and health benefits!

Avoid dopamine piling

We have a tendency to maximise dopamine production by doing many dopamine-stimulating activities together. This is not good for our dopamine baseline. Here are a few tips to avoid dopamine piling and help you maintain more stable dopamine levels:

- Go to the gym or get out into nature without music or a podcast.
- Watch a movie without scrolling on your phone at the same time.
- When watching TV, only watch one or two episodes – not the entire season.
- When you do snack, enjoy one snack fully instead of surrounding yourself with different goodies.

We are all unique and have different needs; there is no one-size-fits-all solution when it comes to things like exercise and movement. Instead of strictly following a workout regime I would like to invite you to look at how different movement makes you feel afterwards. Do you feel energised by what you do?

Is there free, unrestricted movement your body is craving? Is there a form of movement that brings you joy? If you love to play tennis or ballroom dancing energises you with joy, do that! However, by challenging yourself to try new types of exercise, you are also doing your dopamine system good. For me, heavy weightlifting is not something that feels inviting. But, because of the immense health benefits (especially for women over 40) I am going to give it a shot. It's important to do things that challenge us for our pain–pleasure balance.

Embrace the cold

In my home country, Finland, swimming in a hole in the ice is an integral part of the culture. Either you just go swimming in a hole in the ice, or you rotate between the extreme heat of a sauna and cold-plunging or rolling in the snow. Even children are taught to dip into the cold water or roll in the snow and alternate with a sauna.

There are immense health benefits for cold plunging. Many athletes use cold water to decrease inflammation after a heavy workout or a game. Cold-water immersion decreases inflammation and can also help with conditions such as arthritis. Better immune system functioning and increased cardiovascular health are both linked with cold-water immersion. It can also help to balance your nervous system; if we are wired up, it can help us to calm down and feel more grounded.

From dopamine's perspective, cold-water immersion is a powerful activity. A cold plunge can boost dopamine up to 250 per cent above the dopamine baseline, and it can sustain high levels for up to three hours after the plunge. Compare that to chocolate which can increase dopamine 50 per cent above baseline, and sex, which can increase dopamine 100 per cent above baseline.

There are also times when cold-water plunging may not be good for you. Cold-water immersion always causes a stress reaction in your body. This means that, if there is a lot of stress in your life, cold-water immersion can increase your stress levels rather than reduce them. Stress is always cumulative. If you've had a long, stressful period in your life and there are multiple factors causing you mental or physical strain, cold immersion may not give you the health benefits you are looking for. Listening to your body is important.

Building a Life Pulsating with Energy

Resetting your dopamine levels and getting to the root cause of your destructive behaviour is not, by any means, an easy task. The bigger the pain, the greater the pleasure afterwards. And to let go of the things that cause you pain can be scary. So many of the things we incorporate into our lives to shield ourselves from pain become intrinsic to what we believe is our identity, our personality, our core. It can be a relationship, a job or a complete lifestyle. I, myself, have many times felt afraid to let go of the very things that are causing me pain, because, if this too is taken from me, what will be left of me? Leaving the comforts of the known and stepping into the realm of the unknown is scary.

You are capable of building a life pulsating with positive energy – a life where you feel truly alive. There is so much potential lying hidden in you. It's the courage to take the first step that will fill your heart with purpose and meaning, and this will give dopamine a direction to flow – filling your heart and nourishing your soul.

But, it starts with you taking the first step into the unknown and starting an adventure of your own.

Too many of us fear to answer the call of adventure. As a result, we live on autopilot. However, breaking free from this cycle is not only good for your soul, but also your dopamine system. When you explore and engage with the things that you find meaningful, your dopamine system activates. This is the joy of following your own inner path, turning a new page every day and surprising yourself.

Following your own curiosity and stepping away from the road that was built *for* you (but not necessarily *by* you), may be the most courageous thing you can do. By navigating your own path, you are nourishing your soul and building a life of meaning and true purpose.

It's time to dive into the deeper essence of dopamine, starting with how you can consistently move towards a life full of energy, ease and joy.

According to science, the dopamine system has the capability to reset itself: by taking a complete break from the addictive source of our pleasure. Taking a 30-day break from whatever it is that the person relies on can help the brain to readjust its dopamine levels. It can be anything from social media to sugar, to gaming and porn. The first two weeks of this type of break are the hardest – this is the time we might feel the lowest we have ever felt, and that our situation is hopeless. However, usually after two weeks the dopamine balance starts to reset itself – and with it, life starts to look brighter. Resetting your dopamine system and learning to let go of an addictive substance or behaviour is hard work when elements like sleep, nutrition, stress management, social support and trauma work should all be taken into consideration.

We will explore stress management and trauma more deeply in Part Two. For now, I would like to invite you to look at yourself and your behaviour with curiosity and compassion. Is there a behaviour or a substance that you can't seem to let go of? What emotions lie behind these behaviours?

Chapter 2

Joy – Your Compass to Purpose

In the last chapter, we looked at how we stimulate dopamine, and the reward system that we are surrounded by. We also learned a more spiritual meaning of how dopamine gives us direction in life and how living out of alignment with your deeper self can be detrimental to your health and well-being. Now, let's turn our attention to joy – your ultimate guide to purpose and sustainable dopamine.

We are built to explore and move towards things that are meaningful for us. Listening to your heart and finding your way back to your soul's path is not always easy. The first step to help you is to connect with your joy.

The power is not in the destination; the power lies in the path. And finding your way back to joy will guide you towards your own path of meaning and purpose.

When you lose touch with what brings you joy, you close the gate to the immense possibilities that sustainable dopamine sources can bring to your life: a continuous feeling of positive energy and motivation and a sense of tingling excitement in your lower belly. Though the full spectrum of emotions is valid and essential – after all, it's unrealistic to build a life where there is no sadness, anger or envy – joy plays a unique role in allowing us to find deeper value and richness of experience in our life. Joy gives us the energy to get back on the path hidden from us and take steps to our true purpose.

I believe that with the guidance of joy, many artists, musicians and athletes have found their way to meaning. When you are in the presence of a person who is doing what they love, you often feel a surge of energy in your own cells. A key intention for your dopamine living from here on is to see how you can consciously bring more joy into your day to day. It doesn't have to be purposeful or work-related – every fleeting moment of joy, as long as it's fully noticed, counts in terms of balancing your dopamine baseline.

Do you remember the last time you felt like you were exactly in the right place, doing what you were meant to do? Maybe you can remember the joy you experienced while losing yourself completely in the flow of whatever you were doing. This is your direct access to healthy, sustainable dopamine. As a child, I loved building small businesses and organising events. I loved sports and competed in track and field. I loved being in my imaginary world, dreaming about standing on stage and entertaining people. Yet ten years ago in my work, I had none of the elements present that had brought me joy as a child. Maybe that was why I felt so out of place in the world and in myself: I had lost the connection with my joy and the core of who I truly am.

Is there something you could do today just for the sake of joy? Maybe you lose yourself in the 'doing' and become present when you bake. For others, it might be photography, sewing or drawing. Or maybe you find joy in gardening and immersing your fingers deep into the soft black soil.

Over to you

If you feel like you don't have energy or a sense of positive drive in your life, ask yourself the following questions:

- What lights up your heart and excites you?
- Is there something that makes you forget the passing of time?
- Was there something that you enjoyed doing as a child but no longer do? Did you have activities that made you lose track of time? Could you incorporate these elements into your everyday life?

Joy gives you the necessary energy to start making changes in your life, getting back on track and walking on your own path of meaning. Perhaps restarting an old hobby like horse riding or dancing is the energetic push you need to bring more joy to your life. Start painting, learn a new instrument, sing out loud in the shower. Don't be afraid of starting – and don't be afraid of being really bad at something to begin with! We are so afraid of failure that it blocks us from experimenting with fun and growth. But you will grow and learn your way to your new role. Like a child's drawing, you are an original piece of art. Don't let the pressure of perfection dim your newfound joy. Start before you feel 'ready'.

Remember to schedule your joy in. Planning joy doesn't need to be a heavy or draining practice; it can be incidental, but it's definitely a conscious mindset. Dance your way to the coffee maker. Start playing padel tennis, join a choir or a local sports team. Be intentional to sprinkle sources of joy into your day.

Here's my *conscious moments of joy* list – what would you add?

- **Use your favourite colours:** Stop and ask yourself whether there is a colour that is calling you today.
- **Listen to your favourite songs on the way to work:** Make yourself a 'joy playlist' of songs that you know lift you up.
- **Walk barefoot on the beach:** If you can, swim in the ocean.
- **Play with and hug your children:** Laughter is a natural dopamine enhancer.
- **Drink tea from your favourite cup:** Light some candles and enjoy your tea with your favourite chocolate.
- **Explore new music:** Novelty can enhance your dopamine response.
- **Sing along:** Dance and move your body freely and allow the music and your physical self to connect with your joy.
- **Start your week with a class:** Go to a Pilates, yoga or a group exercise class with your friends.
- **Buy yourself fresh flowers**: And display them where you can see them while you work.
- **Wear your favourite outfit:** Dress to impress yourself!

For a healthy dopamine baseline, we need multiple sustainable dopamine sources. It's therefore important not to put all our eggs in one basket – we need to diversify our stock portfolio! If one source of joy becomes weaker, we then still have others to keep us healthy and thriving. Also, when we invest our energy only in one block, such as work, we put a lot of pressure on one thing to provide us with enough energy, meaning and joy. We become workaholics, pushing and pushing to ensure that there is always more. This is when the energy created to fuel us starts consuming us. We don't invest as much time in our friends and families. Instead, we work relentlessly for that promotion, always hungry for more success. This is why in a good job, we can put up with a shitty relationship. And why in a good relationship, we have the energy to put up with a shitty job. But if we want to thrive, we need to have many healthy springs of dopamine, all coming from different sources. By investing in multiple sources of joy, you are creating multiple sustainable dopamine streams in your life which equates to more balance.

Share the joy

When there is joy in what you do, energy flows freely. This is why watching live sport or being at a concert feels so great and gives us an energetic uplift – the joy pulsates through every action and note. When you connect with your joy, you not only lift yourself up, but you also lift others around you. Working towards a mutual goal as a group is a powerful stimulus for our dopamine system. This element harks back to its evolutionary function – when humans work together towards a mutual goal, we are more likely to succeed and thrive. So, whether it's a book club, sports team or a cooking class that sparks your joy, sharing it with others is an invitation for even more positive energy and drive.

For many of my patients, being able to express themselves through creativity has been a gateway to joy in their everyday lives, so let's look now at unlocking your creativity.

Discover Your Own Kind of Creativity

Creativity is an innate source of endless dopamine flow. When we follow our inspiration and create, whether it's new solutions, dance moves or routes to work, we are tapped into a sustainable source of dopamine. When you follow your creativity, it brings joy to your life that nourishes not only your brain and body, but also your soul.

Creativity is your own unique way of seeing the world. You use your imagination to come up with original ideas and find new solutions. You use different avenues to express yourself and connect with people. You can use this creativity in business and at work, at home with the kids and in your hobbies – and ultimately, to create yourself.

Creativity is not a special gift saved only for artists. Your brain is built for creativity and for solving problems in new and novel ways. The key is that you need to find your own kind of creativity. But how do you do this?

I've learnt that we all have a creativity that is unique to us. Some of us are thinking creatives, finding new ways to combine thoughts and ideas together. Some of us are speaking creatives, using words and speaking in a creative manner. Or maybe you are a moving creative, using movement to express yourself in different styles. Food creatives approach cooking by conjuring up unusual and surprising combinations, textures, flavours and colours.

For some of us, the creative powers lie in our hands. Maybe you find that drawing, sculpting, painting or doing with your hands is your avenue for creative expression. Or maybe you are a visual creative, having a gift in seeing the big picture clearly and communicating it with others. Whatever the avenue, following the creative language of your soul is a path to joy, pleasure and sustainable dopamine flow.

Studies have shown that, when starting school, most children believe they are creative artists. Yet, within a few years, most kids have lost their capacity to see themselves as creatives. I think this is a sad example of how we often start losing touch with our own creativity – and creative expression – from an early age. We were all born creative, but, as we age, we seem to lose our capacity to think creatively.

There is an interesting study from the late 1960s, commissioned by NASA, that focused on better understanding the development of creative thinking abilities in humans over time. They wanted to know where creativity came from. Was it something that certain people were just born with and others weren't, or was creativity learned thorough different experiences in life? The general systems scientist George Land and his colleague Beth Jarman took on the challenge and studied 1,600 American children from age five upwards, creating a sample of the American population.

The way that Land and his team defined genius was based on how the children used creative imagination to solve problems. What they found was astonishing. Of this group of five-year-olds, 98 per cent qualified as 'genius'. Five years later, when the children were ten-years old, this had decreased to 30 per cent. Five years later, aged 15, the number was 12 per cent. In adults, this 'genius' level was only 2 per cent.

'What we have concluded,' wrote Land, 'is that non-creative behaviour is learned.' He and Jarman attributed this decline in creative thinking and problem-solving to the rigid structure of traditional education systems, which tend to stifle creative thinking in favour of conformity. What Land and his team found from working with children and looking at how the brain works is that there are two kinds of thinking that happen in the brain: one is called divergent thinking (this is imagination and generating new opportunities) and the other is convergent thinking (this is when we are making a decision or a judgement about something, or we are testing or criticising something). Divergent thinking is like the accelerator in a car, and convergent thinking is like the brake.

In his TEDx talk, Land outlines insightfully how, as kids go through the educational system, we teach them how to do these two different types of thinking at the same time. This means that when coming up with a new idea, a person learns to look at and evaluate it at the same time: 'This is crazy!', 'This hasn't been done before, how could it possibly work?' It's like trying to drive with both your accelerator and your brake glued down – you don't really move anywhere. When you look inside the brain the neurons are fighting each other and diminishing the brain-power we have because we are constantly judging and criticising our ideas. Creative thinking, however, lights up the entire brain.

Our ability to be creative and imagine new possibilities never goes away, though. You strengthen it every time you dream. So, to unlock your creativity, turn back to that child inside yourself, tap into your imagination and become a true creative.

By staying true to and nourishing your own type of creativity, you not only contribute to the whole with your own unique perspectives, you are also taking care of a sustainable dopamine source that is always ready to fuel you with creative energy from the inside out.

Unveil your hidden creativity

Too many times the creative outlets that are truly calling our souls are the ones that equally terrify us. So, what do we do? We stay in the familiar box, stay in that unhappy marriage, instead of staying true and nurturing our creativity as the immense internal powerhouse it is. Start treating it with the nourishment and love we give to a new partner. The best thing we can do for our dopamine system is to bring our hidden creativity to light.

Over to you

- Is there a pathway of creativity that keeps calling you but seems too scary?
- Do you have a creativity stemming from you that you keep hidden?

Your hidden creativity is like an energy fuel that you keep behind closed doors. Fear of rejection, showing up, making mistakes . . . Whatever the fear is, I want to assure you, the energy that you can gain from being true to your creativity is worth it. When we open one door, another one opens, too, making our hidden creativity one of the ways we can find our path back to more energy and meaning.

When you treat your creativity like a new lover and nurture the relationship, you are building a strong flow of sustainable dopamine from within. And with this, your creativity will have the power to lead you to places you couldn't have imagined. You just have to take the step – and listen to your creativity.

Allow space for creativity

Creativity emerges in between spaces, when we are doing nothing. However, as a culture we have a talent of filling any open space we have. Instead of having sustainable dopamine stemming from everyday creativity, we distract ourselves with content and mindless scrolling, or creating content for likes which is quick-fire and feeds our ever-shortening attention spans. When we are waiting in line at the grocery shop, we immediately grab our phones. When we are stuck in traffic, we start looking for other lanes or get frustrated and mad about the situation. It's as if we no longer have the ability to merely be and to do nothing. When, in fact, doing nothing could be the best thing for your creativity, and thus, your dopamine system.

We need boredom, but we resist it with all our might, with social media, busy to-do lists, toxic productivity – instead of allowing ourselves to rest when we feel tired or sit with our boredom, we often fight it. Resetting your dopamine levels requires space and time. We need empty spaces to roam, mentally and physically. We all, children and adults, need free space for new ideas to emerge. Play and creativity – along with sustainable dopamine – thrive only in boredom.

How to break up with your phone

Think back to/imagine a time pre-smartphone, when people weren't as reachable 24/7 and our lives were mostly lived offline. Life was inherently slower. However, creating more distance between you and your smartphone is not always easy. Sometimes you can have withdrawal-like symptoms from not continuously checking your social media feed or inbox for new information. You might even feel a pressing urge to go on your smartphone just to 'do' something. This is your brain and body seeking that fast dopamine hit it has been accustomed to.

Whether you're reading something for work, enjoying a peaceful walk in the park or watching a captivating movie, try to be 100 per cent *in* it, rather than distracted and automatically pulling out your phone. Allow yourself to be fully present, aware and curious about the moment. You can try placing your smartphone out of sight when you don't need it. You can also try deleting any social media apps from your home screen, to make mindless, almost automatic scrolling less easy. You can even place a sticky note on top of your phone, saying 'why am I using my phone?' to remind you to be aware of whether you are picking up your phone to do something important or to distract yourself out of habit.

Reject autopilot

Have you ever noticed how, as if automatically, your hand grabs your phone and clicks open on an app? Or how you take your phone to the bathroom with you, and suddenly, you have spent 20 minutes on the toilet? Our smartphones, with their games and social media platforms, have become a source of fast, unsustainable dopamine 24/7 at arm's reach. According to a survey from Reviews.org, Americans check their phones an average of 144 times a day. People in the UK check their smartphones, on average, every 12 minutes. Two in five adults (40 per cent) look at their phone within five minutes of waking up. We spend a lot of time on our screens. But it is so ingrained in our behaviour now that we don't even notice it. This is a challenge for our dopamine system, as it is continuously bombarded with stimuli.

As a result, we have a hard time concentrating, and we feel stressed more easily. Even hearing a notification signal on our phones can elevate stress hormone levels. Some studies even suggest that seeing your phone releases stress hormones into your system. We are continuously exposed to blue light emitted by smartphones, which interferes with the body's natural sleep–wake cycle. We unconsciously compare ourselves to others on social media, which can contribute to low self-esteem and feelings of inadequacy.

On top of this, because our phone and social media usage is providing us with a continuous stream of fast dopamine through likes, new information and fast transitions, we not only experience the myriad emotional impacts of this through envy, comparison, self-doubt, anger and general unhappiness (we will talk more about the status impact of social media in Part Two), but we also experience withdrawal symptoms when not spending time on our phones, in a negative feedback loop.

Learn to cherish brief moments of stillness by embracing microbreaks away from technology throughout your day. Stare out of the window at the sky. Open the door and look at the nearest tree. Listen out for the sounds of your neighbourhood. These small pauses can work wonders for your well-being and creativity.

Being bored is an invitation for creativity. Leave your phone in the drawer and lean into the notion that feeling bored is not only good for you, but also helping you to create a life filled with more meaning and greater joy.

Little by little, you create more empty spaces in your days. Soon, you may notice how your brain starts to wander and explore new thoughts and ideas. You may daydream and wonder. Not doing anything allows your brain to make new neural connections and spark new creative insights and solutions to problems.

If you find yourself living on autopilot, even small creative acts can give you the energetic push you need. I call these small actions of creativity 'everyday creativity'. Everyday creativity is a powerful way to take care of your dopamine system.

Each time you choose to do things differently, it's an energetic nudge to your system and helps to clear up the foggy feeling of living on autopilot. Listen to a new kind of music. Choose a different route to work. Start a new hobby. Use your non-dominant hand to brush your teeth. Small things, yes, but novel experiences for the brain. And everyday creativity – and sustainable dopamine – at work.

Using Your Superpowers is Your Responsibility

Part of finding joy again is identifying your superpowers – your own unique gifts that take you in the right direction. When you connect with your superpowers, time often flies. You may find that doing these activities takes you into a state of ease and flow. You are aligned with your natural talents and passions. Your superpowers bring you joy and fuel your creativity, making you feel that you are where you should be.

When you spend your energy aligned with your superpowers, you don't become tired the same way as you would when doing other activities. Instead of draining your energy, spending more time doing these activities is often a *source* of energy.

As children, we naturally did the things that excited us and we felt passionate about, but many of us never use these superpowers in adult life. Maybe you loved to create imaginary worlds as a child, but don't really express this imagination in your present life. Or maybe you are a gifted painter, but instead of painting and expressing yourself with colours and shapes, you spend your days in the corporate world, not really connected with your playful and creative side. Maybe at work you feel frustrated that you are doing more and more administrative tasks, instead of spending time with the customers and gathering information to further develop your services. Or maybe you spend your days on autopilot, not connected with what you do. You feel bored and like you are wasting your time. These are both often signs that you are not connected with your superpowers.

Your superpowers are inviting you to tap into the immense potential in you. If you want to find ways to grow and expand into all that you are, sit down and ask yourself: *What are my superpowers?* They are in you, waiting to be explored.

Over to you

Discovering your superpowers is like going on a journey within and finding out what makes you truly exceptional.

- What gives you energy? And what takes it?
- What do you want to be remembered for?
- What do you enjoy doing?

Instead of living life on autopilot, finding ways to incorporate your unique superpowers into your everyday life can boost your days with energy and sustainable dopamine. You'll have a feeling that you are truly alive! With your superpowers, you are inviting creativity and meaning into your life.

Using your superpowers for a greater good

Dedicating your unique superpowers to serve others and create positive change in the world is the surest path to uncovering your deeper purpose and fulfilment, and a lasting flow of sustainable dopamine. It took many twists and turns for me to get to a place in my career where I can use all my superpowers for greater good. I needed to have the courage to trust my gut and follow the beat of my own heart.

I thought for a long time that my medical training would go to waste in Finland. In my home country, the opportunities to practise holistic medicine were limited, and it seemed that many colleagues were also afraid to do things differently from the usual. However, a couple of years ago, I made a big decision and decided to listen to my heart. I wanted to create a space where the patients were treated holistically, focusing on healing the symptoms and the root causes behind them.

The journey is just beginning, but I finally feel that I am in a role where I can utilise my own superpowers: connecting things in a new way, using creativity, as well as my experience as a doctor and my passion for holistic well-being.

Rediscovering joy, finding your own creativity and using your superpowers are the compass to your own unique path of meaning. If your days are filled with feelings of restlessness, depletion or frustration with your life, it can be a sign that you are not spending enough time on your own path. In fact, maybe you are on someone else's path entirely.

In the next chapter, we'll look closely at whether you are following your soul's direction and, if not, how you can rediscover your inner path.

Chapter 3

It Takes Courage
to Follow Your Path

In the last chapter, we explored how joy and creativity are the gateway to your direction and purpose; how they are the first steps to unlocking your dreams, connection and meaning. Now, let's dive a little deeper into your sense of purpose and how to build a life that feels wholeheartedly like *yours*; a life that excites you to your core.

When you are living a life of purpose, you are fuelled by dopamine to take action – even the scary first leap into the unknown. With every step you take, you feel more alive and more aligned with your true self. Dopamine is guiding you in the right direction.

Purpose helps you to find your own place in life. Too often we follow the manuscript someone else has given to us, trying to force meaning on something that doesn't set our souls on fire. We try our best to rationalise how taking the soul-sucking job is the 'smart' thing to do. Or how not expressing our authenticity as fully as possible 'is better for everybody', and we keep ourselves small. This lack of purpose will soon poke an imaginary hole into the dopamine pipe, making your sustainable dopamine leak. However, when you learn how to add more purpose into your days, you can repair these holes and increase the sustainable dopamine flow and positive energy in your system.

Be aware though, finding your purpose in life will take you on an adventure; an adventure in living life to its fullest! Building a world where you are dancing to your own beat and you feel there is intention and meaning in your work (and play) starts with reconnecting with your dreams.

Take Your Dreams Seriously

When we're little, we're not afraid to imagine new worlds and dream freely. However, soon, the people, culture and norms around us start moulding us into boxes, telling us what is possible and what's not. We lose the connection with our dreams, and we create fears and beliefs that start limiting our expressions. Soon, our dreams seem too big or out of line. We stop listening to the whispers from our souls. And, as a result, we start going in the wrong direction.

I was born in a small village in the Finnish countryside. I dreamed about many things – living on the other side of the world, in Hollywood, performing on big stages. I dreamed about leaving a mark. More often than not, though, my dreams felt so different from those around me that I learned to keep my mouth shut.

As I grew older, I started carrying other people's dreams on my shoulders. I remember that I was often dressed in a doctor's outfit as a child. It became part of the tapestry in the stories that I started telling myself. Maybe I should become a doctor. I did love chemistry and science, and I had a sense of approval from my parents when applying for medical school instead of pursuing a degree in the arts. The people and world around me affected the stories I told myself and, eventually, the direction my dreams took me, too. Instead of following the direction of my own heart, I was relying on others to show me my path.

The stories we tell ourselves shape our world. They affect how we interpret situations at work, what we pay attention to at a party, how we perceive a smile on a person's face, how we react to people and events around us and what motivates us to take action. And stories set the desired goals for dopamine.

As Dr Daniel J. Siegel, the world-renowned neuropsychiatrist and author describes in his book *IntraConnected*, the stories we tell ourselves are the foundation of our sense of self. We learn these stories from the people and culture around us. We learn what is a desirable profession and how a good person behaves. We learn what we should aim for. We learn what we should become.

Slowly, with the help of these stories, we become who we are in the world: the good spouse, the boss, the unsure dreamer, the creative one. An energetic and emotional state accompanies these stories. Soon, we feel more ourselves with certain stories than others. They just feel more comfortable.

This sense of self is formed in a part of the brain called the 'default mode network' or DMN. The neural connections of the DMN can be seen as the brain's way of constructing a narrative self. We use stories to create and organise mental models of self that we then carry within us over time. The stories we tell guide our actions, and our actions strengthen our stories. Sometimes we get so caught up with old stories that we start building our future from the past. The well-known saying often attributed to Einstein, 'Insanity is doing the same thing over and over and expecting different results,' is a good phrase to remember. If you are always behaving in the same way, you can't expect different results. Old keys won't open new doors. You need to be open to free yourself from the past and the stories you are telling yourself – and dare to dream from the future.

Foundational stories give us structure and create rules for our lives, but they are not necessarily true (or of benefit to us in any way!). If you pause for a second, can you think of a foundational story that you have carried with you into the present moment? A foundational story might sound like: 'I can have good things in life only after working hard for them,' 'I am not clever with money and need someone else to take care of it' or 'I don't have what it takes to be successful in business.' In all of these stories, there is a belief that is limiting you from living your life to the fullest.

Over to you

Take a moment to reflect on the past stories, experiences or beliefs that no longer serve you. Write them down on a piece of paper, one by one.

Once you have written down the stories you are ready to let go, take the paper outside and safely burn it as a symbolic act of releasing and letting go of these past narratives.

This practice of acknowledging and setting free old stories can be a powerful way to shift your mindset and open yourself up to new possibilities. Take your time with this exercise and be gentle and compassionate with yourself throughout the process.

When your dopamine is following a false direction, you will never feel totally fulfilled and present. You may feel restless, always on the search for the next thing; the next shopping fix, the next promotion, the next social media post, the next hottie on Tinder. This feeling of restlessness is a calling to pause and redirect yourself. Without a connection to your true purpose, this unsustainable dopamine boost is fleeting. As we explored in Chapter 1, soon after you've experienced the high, you may start feeling empty and restless again. When the direction for your dopamine system comes from outside, your life becomes a storm where each wave is followed by a deep drop.

By identifying the stories you tell yourself, you can let go of the subconscious beliefs that no longer benefit you and give dopamine a new direction to flow to. We need to provide our own inner north star – following the coordinates of others simply veers us off-course. When we are connected to our own purpose in life and are moving towards the direction of our own soul, we have a sustainable dopamine flow stemming from inside us. This is the wisdom of dopamine – it can guide us in the direction we should take our lives.

The route back to hearing the voice stemming from my own heart wasn't easy. I was already in my forties when I got my first lead role in the Finnish hit comedy *Like Mother, Like Daughter*. Acting had been a source of joy and a dream since childhood. When I was living in Los Angeles in my twenties, I took steps toward my dreams and started taking acting classes. Acting freed my creativity and made me feel fully present, alive and free. It gave me a chance to bring the stories and characters inside me alive. But I dropped the dream when I moved back to Finland because I felt that, as a medical doctor, it wasn't something I could pursue. For some reason, I was afraid that it would take away my credibility.

Five years ago, while writing about the importance of being true to our dreams, I realised that acting was still something I secretly dreamed of. I also realised that my ex-boyfriend's words, 'You don't have what it takes to act,' were still haunting me. His opinion was so blunt that it had cut away the wings of my acting dream before I truly even tried to fly.

Realising that it was time to take concrete steps towards my dreams, I decided to do a couple of rounds of Emotional Freedom Technique (EFT), which I will teach you in Part Two (see page 157) so you, too, can release old fears that are stopping you from going after your dreams. Within three days, my phone rang – I was asked, out of the blue, to audition for one of the lead roles, the fearless and feisty Jasmine, in the series. My heart was bouncing with joy, but my fears were also kicking in: 'What about my credibility as a doctor? What if I suck at it?'

But I decided to practise what I preach and follow my soul's direction. I took a step back and asked myself: *Am I dancing to the beat of my own heart – or is the song someone else's?* I practised the lines with my teenage daughter, went to the audition and got the role. It became a wonderful experience surrounded by an amazing crew and an act of purpose to show my daughter and everyone else that we don't have to fit into a box.

Over to you

Maybe you can remember when you lost your spark? When you felt like you had missed the train and were left at the station only to see others moving towards their dreams and achieving their goals.

- Can you remember who you were before you learned from the world who you should be?
- What hobbies, creative pursuits or career paths did you have an interest in earlier in life that you had to set aside due to practical or financial constraints?
- Are there any creative, educational or personal growth goals you've always wanted to pursue, but haven't had the chance to, such as learning a new language or immersing yourself in a cause you care about?
- What relationships, connections or communities would you invest more time and energy into nurturing and strengthening if money was not a factor?
- What would your dream career or business be, and how would you spend your days pursuing that path?

You may be coming to the realisation that you have strayed away from your unique path in life. Maybe you have been telling yourself someone else's story or have given up on your dreams. It's also important to remember that sadness and challenges are part of life and all emotions serve a purpose. But you can use joy as your compass and dreams as your map to find your way back from the bottom.

Not being aligned with your deeper self and following your heart causes strain on your system; the subconscious stress starts to wear out your mind, body and soul. For a sustainable flow of dopamine, you need to have a direction of your own. To get there, it's important to be clear about what matter most to you – to identify your core values.

Identify Your Values

Your soul is hungry for authenticity. When you are authentic in your work and personal life – when you are aligned with your core values – you're more engaged and, therefore, tackle tasks and day-to-day life with more energy.

Take some time now to identify your core values. I've listed a few examples below to get you started, but please do research some others that may resonate more with you personally, to create your own core values list:

- authenticity
- balance
- compassion
- creativity
- determination
- fairness
- honesty
- justice
- kindness
- learning
- loyalty
- meaning
- optimism
- popularity
- reputation
- security
- spirituality
- stability
- trustworthiness

- wealth
- wisdom

Having identified your core values, think now about what motivates you overall in your life. Is it:

- Close relationships with friends and family?
- Personal freedom and autonomy?
- Working for the common good?
- Doing things that bring you joy and also lifts up other people?
- Building a lasting legacy?

As we've seen, meaning drives dopamine. This is why working in a job that you don't feel connected with, that doesn't align with your core values, or performing tasks only for others can actually be harmful for your dopamine system. When you are following your own authentic path, you are building a healthy dopamine system that flows in balance from your daily actions.

Over to you

Take some time to really consider whether your current life and work situation align with most, or all, of your core values. And, if not, in what way/s is it out of alignment? Are you in a relationship that drains all your energy? Or are you in a job not aligned with the life you want to build? Maybe you find yourself living more on social media when, in fact, you would like to feel more connected with your life in the here and now? These can all be signs that you need to realign your steps and clarify your direction.

Sometimes we stay in situations that do not support the life we want to build, and our daily actions are not aligned with the direction of our soul. I loved being in love, which for me, in the past, meant merging myself with the other person, becoming *what they needed me to be*. In many ways, I lost myself and instead willingly became the side act, the supporter, the cheerleader for their dreams, trying to be the best possible partner.

Is there anything you could do to bring yourself *nearer* to your values? Don't underestimate how much your small daily decisions impact your long-term health and happiness. Become aware of the daily actions you take and recognise that you need to make intentional changes in your routines so that you are constantly moving in the right direction. Let go of the things that are taking you further away from this path.

What are you doing every day that brings you into closer alignment with, or takes you away from, your core values? If you don't think you are currently doing enough and feel disconnected from your values, start by choosing what you want to have more of in your life.

For example, if close friendship is a core value for you, yet you feel you have lost touch with some of your dearest friends and aren't sure why, could you call an old friend? Create a new WhatsApp group of your closest friends to share memories and current news? Write an old-fashioned letter? Arrange the mates weekend away you've been talking about for years?

When you focus on the small actions you take consistently, you can bring a sense of meaning and intention to even the tiniest actions in your life. When you bring intention into your daily decisions and decide what you want to invite more of into your life, you can ensure that your steps are aligned with the direction of your soul – and that dopamine is flowing in the right direction.

After I paused and became radically honest with myself, it was as if my dreams came back to clarity underneath some dust. I had never stopped believing in them; they were just cramped with a ton of other people's dreams I was unknowingly also carrying in my heart. With every step I took towards them, my dreams were pulsating more and more with life and fuelling my growth.

What is the gift you leave to the world?

In the end, what brings us meaning is not what we end up doing for ourselves, but how we can help others around us. Do you want to be remembered as a present parent? A good friend? Maybe you want to be remembered for the work you did to benefit your local community or the world as a whole? Or maybe you want to be remembered as a person who stayed true to their dreams and had the courage to fearlessly create their own path?

My surgeon friends have told me that they don't really get tired by their long hours, because they find what they do meaningful. The same goes for the athletes I've worked with. They train long hours and give their best on the football field or ice hockey rink, time after time. It's often when professionals lose touch with their meaning, and why and for whom they are doing all of this, that their jobs start to drain them. As Pablo Picasso once famously said: 'The meaning of life is to find your gift. The purpose of life is to give it away.'

When we find and use our gifts, and share them with the world, we are not only doing good for ourselves, but to everybody around us.

But what if you have ignored your inner voice for so long that you can't recognise its whispers anymore?

Every time you feel lost, you can rest safe in the knowledge that your path will reveal itself to you. Trust your dreams and your joy. The wisdom of dopamine is asking you to find your own direction and create your own path.

Over to you

Before we close this chapter, I want you to turn your attention to the new stories, experiences and beliefs you are open to welcoming into your life. Write them down on a fresh piece of paper.

Place this paper somewhere visible, such as on your desk or refrigerator, as a reminder of the positive and empowering stories you are ready to embrace going forward.

Your dreams are your responsibility, and I believe that you should take your dreams seriously. Not only are they a way to get your dopamine system back to balance by providing dopamine from the depths of your being, but dreams are also deeply connected to your purpose. When we stay true to our dreams, the road leading us to finding our purpose can emerge.

Listening to your heart and following your dreams takes courage. To follow one's own beat and not dance to the beat of others can, at times, feel lonely. However, every time you jump, a parachute emerges. It is as if by taking your dreams seriously and betting on yourself, you suddenly see opportunities and solutions you didn't see before. And as the way emerges, so does your own path of purpose, meaning and sustainable dopamine.

In the next chapter, we'll look at how you can make your dreams come true.

Chapter 4

Make it Happen

In the last chapter, you identified your values and rediscovered your dreams, taking another step on your true inner path. And every step that aligns with your core values and dreams supports the sustainable flow of dopamine. In this chapter I want to explore the tools that will enable you to make your dreams come true.

Become the Director of Your Own Life

When it comes to changing your dopamine sources from short-lived, unsustainable ones, to long-lived, sustainable sources, manifesting your future and creating a life where you feel fully alive, neuroplasticity is one of the key concepts underlying the entire process. Neuroplasticity is the brain's ability to learn and create new neural connections. Where attention goes, energy flows.

The brain is a habit machine, trying to save energy wherever it can and choosing the most used pathways. You can imagine your brain as a snowy slope. Every thought you have is like a ride down that hill on a pair of skis – each time you have a thought and glide down the slope, you leave a trail behind in the snow.

The first ride in the fresh snow takes energy and work. But the next time, your skis fall into the previous tracks. And with each slide down, the ride gets easier and faster – and the tracks get deeper. After some time, the tracks are so deep you don't even see the slope anymore.

Neuroscientists propose that we have approximately 70,000 thoughts a day. We can use this creative power to change our lives – and to recreate ourselves. Think of how deep the tracks get when you take the same route for years on end. These neural pathways manifest as different thoughts and emotions. This is why, through repetition, certain thoughts and beliefs become, literally, ingrained into our brains.

When there is a change in your life, your brain becomes more plastic. This means that, when you change workplace, move into a new apartment or have a baby, you can create new neural pathways in your brain more easily. When you use this biological mechanism intentionally to move towards your dreams, you are not only recreating yourself, but also creating a life of your dreams.

When you start choosing different ways of doing things and looking at yourself, it often feels hard at first. Remember, creating a new route takes more energy than following an old path for the brain. You will most likely notice the inner critic in your mind trying to convince you not to put that new dress on or to take your space at the work meeting. Maybe you can even feel your heart beating faster or your palms sweating just thinking about it. But don't worry. Every time you choose a different path, the new route becomes stronger and stronger. Soon, the new way of doing things feels more natural than the old way.

Through practices such as vision boards, visualising your future self or imagining positive outcomes in your everyday life, you may be able to create and strengthen new neural pathways, which then reinforce positive mental patterns that are in alignment with your dreams.

Make a vision board

Our reticular activating system (RAS), which acts as a filter in the brain, determines which information from the environment gets processed and brought to our conscious attention. When we focus our attention on specific goals or desires through practices like visualisation and vision boards, we can potentially prime the RAS to notice relevant opportunities and resources that align with our intentions. It's as if we can see the things we truly want more clearly.

Maybe you can recall suddenly seeing more of your dream car in the traffic than normal. Or if you are hoping to have a family, you may suddenly start seeing more pregnant women and babies around. If you are ready for a loving relationship, you may have a feeling that all you see is couples holding hands. These are great examples of how our RAS filters out information that is meaningful for us. When we consciously 'see' something that is determined as meaningful and important by our brain, our dopamine system has a goal – a direction to flow to. And with a vision board, you can teach your brain what to focus on more frequently.

Before you start creating your vision board, take some time to reflect on your goals and aspirations with the exercise below.

Over to you

What do you want more of? How do you want your career to look? What about your relationships? Where do you want to live? How do you want to spend your days? More than anything, try to focus on the feeling you are looking for.

Feel your dream with your every cell and become more precise and detailed about what your dream future means in practical terms. So, instead of only noting that 'I want a good relationship,' be clear about what a good relationship means for you. How do you want to be treated? How do you want to feel with your partner? What kind of activities would you like to do together? Write down your intentions and clarify what you truly want to manifest. With every clarified intention, you make it easier for energy to flow in that direction.

Next, close your eyes and visualise each of your goals as if they have already been accomplished. Engage all your senses to vividly imagine yourself living the life you desire. Feel with your every cell the sensations when your dreams have come true. How does it feel in your home? How do you carry yourself? What are you wearing? How do you spend your time? How does it look around you? Who are you with?

Now, start gathering materials that resonate with the dream future and emotions you uncovered in the exercise above. Collect magazines, newspapers, photos, quotes and any other items that bring up feelings and emotions that you associate with your dreams. Explore different sources of inspiration and trust your intuition when you collect materials.

Remember, you are defining the emotional frequency for your dreams. Choose with your heart.

When you are ready, find a nice location where you have the mental space to lose yourself in the creative process. Play your favourite music, light candles or do other rituals that help you to set the correct mood for visualisation.

Arrange your selected images, words and symbols on a poster board in a way that feels visually pleasing and inspiring to you. Trust your instincts and allow your creativity to flow as you design your board.

Once your board is complete, place it in a location where you can see it regularly, such as on a wall in your bedroom or your office. Every time you glimpse your vision board, you can connect yourself with the vision you've created and rewire your brain to notice what you truly want for your future.

Try value tagging

Sometimes you don't have the time to sit down and do an entire vision board. In my own life, I use sticky notes! I write down a dream I want to come true, then place these small notes around my apartment. This practice is called 'value tagging'. Just like vision boards, value tagging is an easy way to help your brain to stay connected with your future dreams.

With value tagging, never refine too much. Can you find the essence of your dream? For example, with this book, I simply wrote 'To find the best publisher.' I didn't refine how it should be done or highlight one publisher over another. My dream was simply to find the best home for this book – so I did.

You don't need to find the perfect moment to start creating your vision board. Begin today. Write down what you want in your life. Every practice you do trains your brain to create a future, not from your past, but from the future; aligned with your dreams, values and life itself, giving a steady foundation for sustainable dopamine.

Connect with your future self

When you do the work and realign with your deeper self and your dreams, you don't need to know *how* things will come to life or *what* specifically will happen. The main thing is that you start by spending, even if small, moments experiencing how you will feel in the future with your every cell already in the now. As you take your steps, you can trust that the rest will follow.

Write a letter from your future self

The practice of writing a letter from your future self is a powerful exercise that can help you gain clarity into the kind of future you want to create. You also gain perspective that can help you look at things as positive challenges instead of scary obstacles. At its best, writing a letter from your future self can bring you a boost of positive energy and motivation to recreate yourself – and your life.

First, set the scene. Find a quiet and comfortable space where you can focus without distractions. Set the intention to connect with your future self and gain insights that will guide you on this inner journey.

Next, close your eyes and visualise yourself at a future point in time. This could be one year, five years or even ten years from now. Imagine yourself living your ideal life, accomplishing your goals and embodying the person you aspire to be. How do you feel? What are you excited about? What have you accomplished? What goals have you achieved? Who are you with? How are they making you feel?

Look at this future self of yours with love and gratitude. You can thank them for their courage to make all the decisions that took them to this exact place. Thank them for keeping true to their vision and moving forward, even though it wasn't always easy. Do you feel inspired by all the hard work this 'future you' has done?

After connecting with your future self, step into their shoes and talk to your current self. What advice would your future self give you right now? What words of wisdom can guide you through any obstacles, doubts or fears you may face?

If you don't have insights immediately, don't worry. Stay focused inwards. When you provide your mind with empty space, more often than not insights come and fill that opening.

Now, grab a pen and some paper and start writing the letter. Begin with setting intentions based on the wisdom your future self shared with you. What actions can you take today to align yourself with your future goals and aspirations? Are there specific steps you can take that will move you closer to your desired future? Write in the first person as if you are speaking directly to yourself. Be honest and compassionate.

Once you've finished writing the letter, read it aloud. Feel the words sinking in and notice how they resonate on a deeper level. You can place your hand on your chest and feel the connection between your present and this future self you want to create. Take the wisdom, place it into your heart and feel inspired to take the steps and let your inner wisdom guide you.

Become your future self

Another small change with big impact is to start living as your future self and making decisions as this person. Living from the future is tapping into the future energy you want to embody. You are aligning your current actions with the future you want to create on a practical level.

When you start acting as your future self, you make decisions based on the goals that your future self has. Aligning with this version of yourself can make it easier to work around the fears and doubts that come when your goal is to realign with your truest self and build a life of your dreams.

Let's say you've always dreamed of starting your own business. However, you are feeling overwhelmed. So, instead of taking concrete actions towards your dream, you stay put, dreaming what it would feel like to be doing what you love and imagining how amazing it would feel to be that person who goes after their dreams. But because you don't take the steps, the gap between you and your dreams stays the same.

Living as your future self can help you to organise your dreams into smaller, more manageable steps. When you clarify your vision, you can sense in your bones how the future you feels. You start making choices like them, maybe setting time aside to contact possible clients or go through the paperwork for setting up the business. What types of clothes does your future self wear? How do they carry themselves? Do they have fresh flowers in their kitchen? How do they take care of themselves?

It can feel odd at first making decisions from the future. This is because you are creating new neural pathways in your brain. You are teaching your brain to feel, act and think differently. This is hard work and it takes energy. However, after some time the process becomes easier and starts taking less energy. This is because the neural pathways in your brain have become stronger.

When you look at each of your choices through your future self, you are teaching your brain new ways of being you, which means that, one decision at a time, this aligned version of you starts feeling more and more, well, like your true self.

If you have difficulties dreaming your future, you can try using this simple mantra: 'What will come will come, what should go will go.' This is a powerful and easy way to create trust and get closer to your path.

Find your people

The people we surround ourselves with significantly influence our well-being and personal growth. We often attract people who make us fall into old, familiar behaviours and dynamics. When we build relationships based on trauma, it's as if the pain is leading us, not love. When we heal old wounds, the pain no longer runs the show. As a result, we get back to alignment with our true selves and start making decisions that are genuinely doing good to us, mind, body and soul.

We will dive deeper into trauma work in Part Two. However, below are some quick tips you can use to help assess whether or not you are building your tribe based on old fears or new alignment:

1. Pay attention to how you feel after spending time with someone. Do you feel energised and uplifted or do you feel drained and depleted? Surround yourself with people who bring positive energy and support your growth.

2. Consider whether you feel free to be yourself and explore your passions and interests around your close circle. It is said that we are the sum of the five people we spend the most time with. Sometimes you just need to bring some fresh and uplifting energy into your inner circle.

3. Appreciate honesty and surround yourself with individuals who provide constructive and honest feedback. People like this challenge you to expand your horizons, question your assumptions and offer valuable insights for personal growth. A true friend tells the truth even though sometimes it might be hard to hear.

4. Our journey is often not about *how* but also about *who*. Reaching goals and daring to dream big is always easier – and more fun – when moving forward together.

Resist the Push and Let it Flow

As you continue the inner work of balancing your dopamine system and finding your way back to your deeper self, it is all about setting the direction and less about the speed. Many of us, myself included, have become so impatient and want to have everything at once.

However, when we learn to resist the push and let energy flow, the results we were looking for can come from unexpected sources and routes we didn't even think about.

As a society, we tend to value ourselves based on how much we are doing, optimising our time and energy. Our lives are continuously stimulated by multiple tabs open on different devices – a ticker tape team of flags waving for our attention and time. We expect to constantly feel energised, and we have been conditioned to loathe laziness. We crave dopamine and meaning, so we continuously work harder to achieve a goal. We strive for perfection and acquire more projects, filling our days with tasks to perform.

We put immense value on the idea of 'pushing' and 'making things happen'. This continuous desire for more is the dark side of dopamine that is driving most of our Western culture and devouring our planet. The need for a bigger home, a better car or a more extravagant everyday life – it can feel highly pleasurable to be in 'push' mode, always working hard to make things better. However, there are interesting studies linking type A personalities (often characterised by competitiveness, time urgency, impatience, hostility and a strong desire for achievement) with higher incidence of heart attacks and cardiovascular disease.

As a slower pace of life is rarely a realistic way of living, we might feel there's no alternative to juggling multiple balls all the time. Pushing and multitasking can give you the sweet rush where you feel you're achieving and 'moving forward'. With its rapid switches between different tasks, it can be a powerful and addictive source of dopamine. Consider how many times you have 'multitasked' your downtime – you know, you're binge-watching Netflix, but you're also scrolling on your phone or (and!) laptop, and mindlessly eating pizza and crisps. That's a dopamine banquet, but the feasting undermines the power of the dopamine you've created.

In the same way, taking on multiple projects at once, for example trying to write an important work email while also focusing on a personal writing project and at the same time taking care of some admin, doesn't necessarily lead to better productivity. When we switch between tasks, there's a 'switching cost' associated with the cognitive effort required to refocus attention and reorient to the new task. So, with the excitement and energy of juggling multiple balls in the air, you also *lose* energy – and can decrease your performance, too. Rapid task-switching and dividing your attention can compromise your working memory and problem-solving skills, as well as controlling your attention, making it difficult to retain information or solve complex problems effectively.

> For a day, try to do one task at a time and finish each one before moving on to another. Becoming more mindful of only doing one thing at a time and completing that fully is an invitation for a more sustainable flow of dopamine. This is not only a great way to achieve a goal, but also an opportunity to lean away from the habit of multitasking.

Your dopamine system is a system of hope. As we saw in Chapter 1, the power of dopamine lies in the pleasure of anticipation; more specifically, the anticipation of something good *happening soon*. But there is *actually* a drop in production once you are in receipt of whatever treasure trove experience you were waiting for. From an evolutionary perspective, dopamine evolved to help us feel motivated to pursue tasks essential to survival: going out in dangerous terrain to forage for food, to build shelter, to seek a mate. You can think of the dopamine system as an evolutionarily ingrained reward system that helps us learn exactly what actions bring us the desired results. This system motivates and gives us the energy to seek and move forward towards the things that matter to us.

Achieving a goal – whether that's getting a cup of coffee, enjoying delicious food, playing video games, having sex or buying a new home – activates the opioid system, which then makes us feel good. However, as the dopamine system is stronger than the opioid system and always wants more, we soon need a new goal.

Dopamine also helps us to feel motivated to work towards rewards that are months or even years away. Our dopamine levels can rise significantly when we even think of a future reward that is uncertain and far away, such as our next summer holiday or retirement. Dopamine fuels us to work for things for the long haul. And the uncertainty about the prize, well, it only excites dopamine. This is one of the reasons why jobs or relationships where you have to constantly push to make things work can be so intriguing for us. The more we push towards a goal and the more we anticipate the desired thing to happen, the more we feel fuelled by the challenge.

As novelty and unpredictability can stimulate the dopamine system, chaos and always having something to work on can act as a way to keep things 'exciting' and help to fuel the thrill of dopamine. Without continuous drama or chaos, it can be hard to feel fulfilled or excited. This constant high level of dopamine makes us feel that we are continuously moving towards our goals. We fall in love with the high of the ride. We try to consume our way to meaning and purpose. 'Normal' becomes boring. We crave the excitement of 'the push'.

However, the push can often lead us to feeling more disconnected and empty than ever and we can't stay in this dopamine-dominant mode for too long. This continuous pushing is how many of us end up burned out. Energetically, we are driving with the accelerator glued to the floor. The ride feels amazing and things are moving fast. However, it is unsustainable. This dopamine dominance over the other love hormones – serotonin and oxytocin – is wearing out the engine and the parts (our body and mind). Instead of giving us the feeling of freedom and joy we so crave, continuously striving for more can enslave us. The strain is too much for the system. I had to learn this the hard way.

Before I learned how to balance my dopamine levels, dopamine dominated all my other love hormones. This tipped the scales on the other end of creativity and energy; without inner peace, my expansive energy didn't have a clear direction. I was like a firework, loud, sparkling and going off in all directions. My behaviour was almost hypomanic.

In this state of hypomania, dopamine is released more strongly in specific brain regions, leading to a heightened sense of reward and pleasure. This means we often become more impulsive and take bigger risks than usual. In business, this can show up as excessive spending or taking on unrealistic projects. We multitask and have multiple balls in the air at the same time. Go big or go home – that is the mentality.

In some environments, such as sport, investment banking, tech and start-ups, this dopamine-dominant state can even be seen as the ideal or celebrated. Our enthusiasm is contagious and people feel inspired around us. This is also good when you want to create a dynamic business environment. People reward us for our good vibes and high energy, creating a positive feedback loop that keeps the hypomanic state going.

We surround ourselves with like-minded grinders, always ready to push for the next big thing: the next big work project, the next investment round, the next goal.

Unable to be in the present, we are constantly planning for a future reality, but never embracing or acknowledging where we *are*. We are escaping the present into the doing. Dopamine's energy blasts forward, but without a sense of acknowledging presence and progress, the great leap you are hoping for doesn't happen.

Maybe you can pinpoint a time in your own life when you fell in love with the push? Maybe you subconsciously or even consciously do lots of things all at the same time, multitasking for the dopamine rush and excitement of having multiple plates spinning? Being in this push mode is often a sign that there is dopamine dominance in your system.

When we are in push mode, we work hard to make things happen. We are used to fighting boredom with social media, busy tasks and to-do lists, but, in fact, just as we saw when we looked at uncovering creativity on page 54, when you are resetting your dopamine system, you need to create space. Often, our dreams are only realised after we learn how *not* to push, instead allowing things to happen.

Ease your grip and trust that everything is unfurling in your favour and that all the right people will emerge into your path just at the right time.

Slowing down

Having the capacity to feel bored, tired and do nothing is your friend. Every time you choose to slow down, to do only one task at a time, to invite more stillness into your life, you are deeply nourishing your dopamine system. More specifically, you are helping your dopamine baseline.

Next time you go for a walk around the block or in your local park, try leaving your phone in a drawer at home and see how it helps you to slow down.

Celebrate Your Accomplishments – Big and Small

Every time you reach your goal, even if it's a small one, it activates your dopamine system. The smaller and more manageable your goals, the more opportunities you have for a constant flow of dopamine. Setting yourself goals that are aligned with your true purpose and then achieving small steps towards them is key for a long-lasting flow of dopamine. Celebrating and truly acknowledging your accomplishments can also provide an immense sense of satisfaction, enhancing your dopamine levels.

Here are some tips and advice for goal-setting and celebrating your successes:

- **Break down goals into manageable steps:** Even the highest mountain was climbed one step at a time. Set yourself achievable, realistic steps and celebrate all the small accomplishments on the way to your goal. One small step often leads to another step and soon, you have created a big change in your life.
- **Take time to celebrate your accomplishments:** Choose rewards that feel like the perfect prize for your hard work, such as treating yourself to a meal at a restaurant you've always wanted to go to or raising a toast with family or friends.
- **Journal and reflect on your achievements:** Make some time to regularly and consciously reflect on your progress and how much you've achieved. I also love having a gratitude jar, where you write something you have accomplished on a piece of paper every week, put it in the jar and read it at the end of the year!

The act of writing down your thoughts, feelings and experiences in a journal or gratitude list can help enhance dopamine release. This is because expressing yourself creatively engages the brain's reward pathways. Reviewing past journal entries and reflecting on your progress and growth can also boost dopamine as you recognise your accomplishments.

Setting journaling goals, such as writing for a certain amount of time each day, provides a sense of achievement when those goals are met, further increasing dopamine.

Making a list of things you are grateful for focuses your attention on the positive aspects of your life. Expressing gratitude activates the brain's reward system, releasing dopamine. Regularly reviewing your gratitude list reinforces those positive associations, helping to maintain elevated dopamine levels. Adding new things to the gratitude list provides a sense of growth and abundance, further boosting dopamine.

Celebrations boost dopamine and reinforce positive behaviours, while goal-setting provides direction and motivation. Finding joy in the process and celebrating both big and small victories can cultivate a positive mindset and a sense of fulfilment. And when your goals are tied into a deeper meaning and into your soul's mission, every step you take lights up your dopamine system.

To have a healthy dopamine system, you also need a strong serotonin system so that all your creative and expansive energy doesn't leak in unhealthy directions, but takes you forward on your soul's path. In the next section, we will be revelling in the warm embrace of serotonin, your hormone of safety, trust and security.

Your to-do list for a healthy flow of dopamine

- Pause daily and ask yourself, 'Is this serving the direction I want to walk?'
- Plan joy.
- Move daily.
- Give space for creativity.
- Dream from the future.
- Take responsibility for using your unique superpowers.
- Pause and think: *how can I use my superpowers to help others in the world?*
- Embrace boredom.
- Write your goals on a sticky note or make a vision board.
- Surround yourself with people who lift your spirit and help you achieve your goals.
- Take the first step even if you don't see the road. Trust that the road will appear.

Part 2

Serotonin: The Hormone of Safety

Chapter 5

What is Serotonin?

Serotonin is dopamine's counterpart. Where dopamine is the wild risk-taker, always looking for something new and loving to stand on the edge, serotonin is about safety and the long game. If serotonin was an investment banker, it would concentrate on low-risk and steady, but also low-reward investments. What is important to remember is that dopamine and serotonin are two sides of the same coin. This means that if you want a flourishing dopamine system, you need to also build strong serotonin scaffolding to support it. Like the balancing aspects of yin and yang, or each side of a seesaw, serotonin and dopamine equally help to create a powerful balance for expansion and personal growth.

Serotonin loves safety, familiarity and feeling valued. It's the keeper of our safety system. Imagine a shield, layering and protecting you – think of serotonin as a protective shield for your energy.

From an evolutionary perspective, we have found safety in being part of a group or a member of the herd. Our biology is wired for belonging and we seek assurance from our relationships with others. We long to belong and feel accepted by our groups.

However, we also have unique tendencies in what actions feel more natural to us within a group. Dopamine-dominant people are built to see fresh opportunities and explore new possibilities. Dopamine-dominant people would have traditionally been the ones to go and seek new camping grounds or go on explorations for new continents. Serotonin-dominant people are motivated by staying put, caring for the village and looking out for potential threats.

At its best, these two can harmoniously work together, building a balance between safety and expansion – both holding on and letting go. This is wonderfully illustrated in successful teams, whether it's a sports team or a group of people at work: having both serotonin-dominant and dopamine-dominant people can help us to work better as a whole.

Serotonin acts as a neuromodulator in the brain, meaning it doesn't just send signals from one neuron to another, but also influences the overall tone or mood of the brain. It's like a conductor in an orchestra, ensuring that all the instruments (or neurons) are playing in harmony, contributing to our overall sense of wellbeing, mood stability and the ability to cope with stress.

When we feel safe, our body shifts from a state of alertness or fight-or-flight to a state of rest-and-digest, which is essential for repair and healing. In this state, serotonin plays a crucial role by enhancing this sense of safety and well-being. It also helps regulate sleep, which is vital for repair and recovery, and modulates our appetite in a way that supports nutritional intake, further aiding in the body's healing processes. Serotonin also influences our pain perception, making discomfort more manageable, and supports the functioning of the immune system, ensuring that our body can effectively repair itself and fend off illness.

The sense of safety and the presence of serotonin work together to create an environment where our body can prioritise healing and regeneration. By signalling to our brain and body that we are in a secure place, serotonin aids in lowering stress levels and inflammation, directing the body's resources towards maintenance and recovery. This harmonious interaction highlights the importance of mental wellbeing in physical health, demonstrating how feeling safe and supported can significantly impact our body's ability to heal and maintain optimal health.

From an evolutionary perspective, serotonin evolved to help us process energy metabolically. Serotonin helps our bodies absorb nutrients and allocate precious energy to the parts of the body where it is most needed; it gives us the energy to grow, repair and heal.

Serotonin is often described as a 'happiness hormone', but this is only half of the story. I believe that serotonin has a deeper meaning, too: it protects our energy. Where dopamine gives direction to your energy, serotonin is there to protect it. When serotonin is in sustainable balance, it is easy for you to set boundaries. You don't scrimp on putting yourself first and listening to your needs. You feel enough as you are, so you are not afraid to spread your wings and fly.

However, when our serotonin levels are not balanced, it causes leaks in our energy, which can show up in several ways.

The Dark Side of Serotonin

When our serotonin levels are low, we might feel a deep sense of unease: we feel more anxious, always waiting for the worst to happen. In this way, an imbalance in serotonin levels can prevent us from enjoying our lives wholeheartedly. Instead of trusting everything will work out, we ruminate on the past or worry about the future. We live our lives on autopilot and can't get a hold of light-hearted joy that bubbles all the way from our gut. When your serotonin levels are low, you don't see all the possibilities in life – your brain focuses more on the risks. As a result, instead of stretching your wings and expanding, you focus on protecting your energy.

For example, you might not leave your soul-sucking job because you are afraid to lose that guaranteed income. Maybe you stay in a withered relationship because you can't afford to live independently. Perhaps you invest too much in activities that are not nourishing your soul. Or maybe you are doing things out of obligation or because 'it has always been this way'. You stay in the familiar because of the sense of safety it brings. You find yourself in a cage, keeping yourself small, imprisoning yourself in false security.

We seek this false security and reassurance of our status from our jobs and relationships. We seek safety by doing what has always been expected of us – the traditions and stories we have learned to love. We overshare online to feel connected. We transgress our own boundaries and integrity, say 'yes' when we want to scream 'no', and feel thwarted and become bitter. Our days are filled with thoughts of what life could look like now if we had just taken that chance.

Have you ever looked at your life and wondered, how the

heck did I end up here? When your body doesn't have enough serotonin or it isn't using the serotonin available effectively, you can find old fears pushing you into things, instead of your future dreams pulling you forward. This is exactly when we look for serotonin and a sense of safety from the wrong places, craving genuine connection and intimacy from where there is none, and getting ourselves into toxic relationships or unhealthy situations.

When I was off balance and had lost my inner safety, I started looking for that security from relationships. That path led me to some very dark places before I understood that true safety had to come from within myself. Those difficult days feel far away now, and I am comfortable sharing my darkest moments in the hope of supporting others who may be struggling to leave toxic relationships. It's an important reminder that anyone, intelligent people, can find themselves trapped in an abusive situation. But no one should stay in one.

My relationship with my ex-boyfriend initially felt so secure, strong and balanced, but, over time, I found myself in a living hell. The fear of losing my freedom and his fear of abandonment created a darkness that brought out the worst in both of us. (This is a great example of how we gravitate towards our fears – in this relationship I ended up losing my freedom, and he ended up being abandoned.) He would break things, control me, restrict me from seeing friends and family, even my colleagues. The verbal abuse was excruciating. I found myself screaming and fighting like an animal. I could no longer recognise myself. Sometimes it felt like I was acting in a movie.

For anyone who hasn't experienced mental or physical violence, this may sound too extreme to comprehend. But due to the process of neuroadaptation, for me, the abuse started to feel almost 'normal'. The cycle of apologies, make-up sex and temporary affection, followed by more abuse, kept me trapped. The spikes of oxytocin (more on this in Part Three) created a false sense of trust that things would improve.

I used to watch movie scenes about relationships with emotional or physical violence and think, 'How could they ever end up there, why don't they leave?' The simplicity of this perspective changed when I found myself living out such a scene. Suddenly, it was me who was in an emotionally volatile and toxic coupling, a relationship where our shadows merged, creating darkness so deep it seemed impossible to escape. My brain became so adapted to the situation that it didn't feel safe to leave. I was the person unable to break free.

What to do if you find yourself in an unhealthy relationship

1. **Recognise the toxicity:** Noticing and looking at the situation with honesty is the first step – and acknowledging that no one should be in an unhealthy relationship.

2. **Gather support:** Even if it might be hard to talk about the situation, finding a friend or a professional to support you and give you strength to get out of the relationship, is essential.

3. **Try to find ways to give yourself nourishment and rest:** Is there a place where you can go and rest if home is not the place for this? Rest can help you see the wood from the trees and envision a way out of the situation. Yoga nidra and meditation can be great tools for this (see pages 160 and 117).

4. **Protect your boundaries:** Is there a way that you can protect your boundaries? See Chapter 7 where we will examine trauma and boundaries.
5. **Create a plan and timeline:** Develop as detailed a plan as possible and try to stick to it. Don't hesitate to ask for help.
6. **Be gentle with yourself:** Progress is rarely linear and there are often setbacks, but there is always light at the end of the tunnel.

Looking back, I can see clearly that my relationship was not healthy – it was dysfunctional, at times abusive, although I didn't fully recognise this until I had the power of hindsight. Any kind of physical or emotional abuse in a relationship is not acceptable, and I would urge others experiencing it to seek help for yourself or others if you recognise any of the elements I've spoken of above.

When we don't have enough serotonin in our system, we don't have the courage to step outside of our comfort zone to grow. We stay in the familiar, even though we know it's not aligned with our true needs. I hope that by telling my story, you have the courage to look at your own life with compassion and recognise where old pain or trauma may be pushing you into unhealthy situations, instead of your own dreams and genuine needs leading the way. Looking back, I realise I ended up in that situation because I had lost my sense of inner safety, and desperately sought external safety within relationships. My boundaries weren't strong enough, and my serotonin was leaking.

When we wrap ourselves in the comforts of false security, we make decisions out of fear instead of love. It's as if pain is steering the ship and affecting decision making. As a result, you continue to build your future based on the past – and your life stays the same. Instead of leaving that toxic relationship, applying for that exciting job or starting your own business, you stay in the familiar because it feels safe. Without a strong serotonin system, we use our precious energy to make other people happy. And, as a result, we feel overwhelmed and depleted, instead of excited and truly alive.

Over to you

- Is there something that resonates with you here?
- Do you feel comfortable being by yourself?
- Deep down, what are you afraid of?
- Are you looking for security from places that keep you trapped?

When life has pulled us down and we have hit rock bottom, it can be hard to see a way out. Whether it's a toxic relationship, a job that fights against your very being, having no money, finding out that you live in a mould-infested apartment or getting scammed, these are all blows to our serotonin system. And when our serotonin system shakes, it strains our nervous system and we can't see the light at the end of the tunnel. When I was in that toxic relationship, my mind kept playing tricks, convincing me that things would change. But the truth is, we can't change the people around us. We can only change and heal the parts of ourselves that resonate with their darkest parts. Similarly, we often see the light more clearly after a very dark moment. That happened to me as I found the strength to regain my freedom – and locate the safety within. As we move forward together and you learn ways to work with trauma in this part of the book, you will also see that you are more able to heal old pain. The stronger your serotonin system becomes, the easier it is for you to find a sense of safety and be engaged by situations that are genuinely nourishing your body, mind and soul.

When you don't face your fears, they will lead you subconsciously to situations that although familiar, are not genuinely good for you. Fear keeps our nervous system activated, and too much activation strains the system. Thankfully, with daily practices, we can affect our sense of safety and also release subconscious stress.

You can use external sources such as tryptophan-rich foods (salmon, eggs, nuts or spinach), massage, sunlight and exercise to support your serotonin levels. However, the secret to a healthy and long-lasting serotonin system comes from doing inner work and creating a strong sense of safety from within. A powerful stream of love hormones is built from the inside out. You can do this by:

- **Shifting your nervous system from fear to safety:** When we have unhealed pain or trauma, these fears create subconscious stress that often affects our sense of safety and, thus, our serotonin system. Once you start to let go of old fears and heal, this strengthens your sense of safety and supports a healthy flow of serotonin from everyday life itself. We'll be looking at how you can face your fears and balance your nervous system in Chapter 6.
- **Recreating healthy boundaries:** Finding ways to strengthen your boundaries in different areas of your life can help you to balance your serotonin system.

Without clear boundaries you can easily end up using your energy to please others, instead of listening to your own needs. Chapter 7 will guide you through practical ways to create healthy boundaries.

- **Letting go of limiting beliefs:** Limiting beliefs are subconscious thought patterns that can stifle our ability to achieve our goals and chip away at our self-worth. In Chapter 8 we'll explore ways to let go of limiting beliefs and strengthen your self-worth as when you build this up it powers your serotonin system. You no longer need to find safety from performing a role; you feel safe enough to express yourself authentically and say what you need out loud.

Life is in constant motion. Shit happens, and we get muddy curveballs thrown our way that bring us to our knees. However, when you understand how your nervous system works, what messages different physical symptoms and emotions may carry and how to balance your nervous system, you have an inner map with you, always guiding you back to safety and connection.

We are about to dive into some inner work that will help you build a stronger serotonin system. Firstly, below are some strategies to nourish your body and mind and help your healing and growth process in the here and now.

Immediate Serotonin Support

Spend time in nature

Just six minutes in nature has been proven to increase our serotonin levels, reflecting the broad and immediate impact of nature on our mental health and well-being. Walking barefoot and touching the soil can further connect you to the earth's natural energy, activate the nerve endings in your feet and support your skin's microbiome – a key component in our body's defence system and overall health.

Nourish your gut microbiome

The gut microbiome, the complex ecosystem of trillions of microorganisms living in the gastrointestinal tract, has a significant influence on serotonin synthesis. Many of the bacteria in the gut possess the enzymes required to produce serotonin from its precursor, the amino acid tryptophan. In fact, the gut is estimated to produce around 90 per cent of the body's serotonin.

The diversity and composition of the gut microbiome can impact serotonin levels. A healthy, balanced microbiome is associated with optimal serotonin production, while an imbalance (dysbiosis) can lead to reduced serotonin levels and potentially contribute to conditions such as irritable bowel syndrome.

Our gut is also intertwined with our emotions – our 'gut instinct'. Your gut health can absolutely affect your mood. Disruptions in gut health can influence sleep patterns and the quality of your sleep. Research has also linked imbalances in the gut microbiota to mood disorders such as depression and anxiety.

There are several things you can do to nourish your microbiome:

- **Clean, nutrient-rich and colourful foods are your microbiota's best friends:** Beneficial bacteria that have the necessary enzymes to produce serotonin from tryptophan thrive on fibre. Without enough fibre, these small helpers will starve and start to eat out the colon lining, leaving the colon vulnerable to inflammation. Fill your plate with vegetables, berries, wholegrains and fruit.

- **Eat both probiotics and prebiotics:** Probiotics are live bacteria and yeasts that can have beneficial effects on your body. These little helpers already live in your body; supplementing them adds to your existing supply of friendly microbes, supporting your health and immune function. Prebiotic foods, such as wholegrains, bananas, greens, onions, garlic and soya beans are high in special types of fibre that support digestive health. They feed the gut bacteria with enough fibre and increase the amount of these friendly helpers. This can aid various digestive problems and even boost your immune system. Prebiotic foods have also been shown to improve metabolic health and even help prevent certain diseases.

- **Keep your alcohol consumption minimal:** Alcohol has a negative impact on the microbiome and it also increases the inflammatory response.

- **Stress shows directly in your microbiome:** When we learn ways to regulate our nervous system we also nourish the good bacteria in our gut.

Move your body

Physical activity can boost the release of serotonin in the brain and enhance the quality of sleep. Movement is medicine in many ways, so try to nourish your body and mind with it whenever you can.

But remember that rest is productive and essential. Without enough rest, our bodies respond with a stress reaction. Research also shows that women need only half the amount of exercise as men for the same health benefits, so sometimes less can be more. Walks in nature are great for everyone and for our serotonin levels!

Stay hydrated

Dehydration can negatively impact serotonin production and function. The amino acid tryptophan requires adequate hydration to be properly converted into serotonin in the brain. Dehydration also increases stress hormones, which can decrease serotonin levels.

Experience the magic of writing by hand

If something is bothering you, put pen to paper and let your thoughts flow freely. The physical act of writing down thoughts and feelings when journaling can help process and release negative emotions. This emotional expression has been linked to increased serotonin release in the brain. Journaling is also a reflective practice that can help alleviate stress and anxiety – and lower stress levels correlate with higher serotonin activity, as chronic stress can deplete serotonin. The simple act of consistently journaling can also provide a sense of structure and accomplishment, which can trigger the brain's serotonin release.

Foods to support your serotonin system

- Consume tryptophan-rich foods, such as eggs, salmon, poultry, nuts and seeds (especially almonds, walnuts and pumpkin seeds), tofu, cheese, legumes and dark leafy vegetables. Tryptophan is one of the essential building blocks in serotonin production.

- Omega-3 fatty acids and vitamin D can also help serotonin production and receptor activity in the brain. Fatty fish, flax seeds and chia seeds are good sources of omega-3s.
- Carbohydrates cause a spike in insulin levels, helping tryptophan cross the blood–brain barrier more effectively. This may be why 'comfort foods' often include some carbs. A piece of chocolate after your meal can also do the trick (and I rarely skip it!).
- Pay attention to how you eat. Taking a moment to express gratitude before starting your meal can help activate your digestive system, setting the stage for better nutrient absorption and serotonin production.

Welcome on your journey to understanding how optimising serotonin can offer you the perfect springboard to adventure as well as security. In this part of the book, you will find out how to seek safety from within instead of relying solely on others to feel safe. You will learn how to set boundaries that protect your energy, and you will come to see yourself as the beautiful, unique and radiant being that you are.

By the end of this part of the book, you should have some instant and some longer-term practices that you can build into your everyday, to ensure that your personal security system is fully charged and in wonderful working order. Get ready to start living the life you've always wanted to lead! This all starts with regulating your nervous system.

Chapter 6

Shift Your Nervous System
from Fear to Safety

Stress is our friend and the body's natural response to per-ceived threats or challenges; we need stress to move forward in life and go after things that are meaningful to us. It involves the release of hormones like cortisol, adrenaline and dopamine to prepare for a fight-or-flight reaction and respond to the situation.

Stress can also operate on an unconscious level, with subtle environmental and psychological factors triggering the stress response without our conscious awareness. This is why isolation and loneliness can make us sick. This is also why childhood trauma can make us overreact to a seemingly normal situation.

Prolonged or chronic exposure to both conscious and unconscious stressors can lead to a state of distress. This chronic stress can disrupt the body's natural serotonin balance, and affect both our body and mind:

- Persistent high cortisol and low serotonin levels
  may damage brain regions involved in mood

regulation, impair immune function and promote inflammation.
- Chronic stress-induced serotonin dysregulation can be linked to mental health issues like anxiety and depression.
- When our coping mechanisms for a sense of safety become overwhelmed by the effects of conscious and unconscious chronic stress, our serotonin-system gets more easily off balance.

Simply put, the situation becomes too overwhelming for us. We feel that we don't have the resources to get what we truly need. We don't have the support or the energy to cope with the circumstances – there is a feeling that it's out of our hands and there is nothing we can do to change the outcome. Stress has become unhealthy.

It's time to work with your mind and body to reduce subconscious stress, create more safety from within, break free from old pain and become the person you were created to be.

Why you need to feel safe to let go of excess weight

Lack of nutrition, excessive exercise or lack of an internal sense of safety can signal a threat to our body, to which the body reacts with a stress response. The fat cells can respond to the lack of safety by accumulating fluid and growing bigger or increasing in number. This is why losing weight can be hard when our body is not feeling safe.

How to Balance Your Nervous System

You can think of the nervous system, also called the auto-nomic nervous system (ANS), as an information channel reaching every inch of your body, connecting your brain, spinal cord and body. The nervous system controls how your body functions, with high-energy states on one end and low-energy states on the other. Its job is to keep you alive and safe. We often think that the immune system sends cells to fight off infection when we are sick. But it is actually your nervous system that tells organs, like your spleen and the immune cells in the bone marrow, to release cells that go and hunt down bacteria and viruses that the system sees as invaders. A well-functioning nervous system is the basis of hormonal balance. This is why a healthy serotonin system starts with a balanced nervous system. When you learn how to balance your nervous system, you are building sustainable serotonin sources on top of a well-constructed and solid foundation.

The nervous system controls all bodily tasks and has two ends: the sympathetic and parasympathetic ends. The sympathetic end activates when we are afraid, preparing us to fight against the intruder, run away and hide or cry for help in panic. When the sympathetic nervous system and the fight-or-flight response activate, you can think of energy intensifying and going outwards to ensure your survival.

The parasympathetic branch, on the other hand, is responsible for restoration – the rest-and-digest response. The parasympathetic state activates when you feel safe. More blood flows into the digestive organs, stimulating digestion and ensuring optimal nutrient intake. Your heart rate slows down and you feel relaxed. Your body is taking energy in and recharging its batteries. This is the state where wounds heal, hair grows and the body detoxes itself faster. When you have a strong serotonin system and a solid sense of safety stemming from within, your nervous system can allocate energy to repairing and healing instead of using it all up preparing to fight or run away and living in survival mode.

The vagus nerve can be thought of as the switch between the sympathetic nervous system's fight-or-flight response and the parasympathetic nervous system's rest-and-digest response. This long and wandering nerve originates in the brainstem and extends through the neck and into the chest and abdomen. The vagus nerve collects information about our internal state and the world around us. Based on the information it gathers, it either activates the fight-or-flight or the rest-and-digest response. This is why knowing how to activate the vagus nerve through exercises like breathwork and movement is an important way to move your nervous system from fight-or-flight to rest-and-digest – and a great way to support your hormonal system.

The state of the nervous system is reflected in your mind and your body. Imbalances in serotonin levels have been strongly linked to panic attacks, but it wasn't until I experienced my own struggles with panic attacks that I truly realised just how profoundly our serotonin levels can impact our body–mind system. The panic attacks seemed to come out of nowhere: at a restaurant in the middle of a pleasant conversation with a friend, during a meeting or when I was on stage giving a speech. And the more afraid of the panic attacks I became, the more likely they were to start. My heart would start racing, the blood would run out of my limbs and I'd feel like I was going to faint right there and then. I was so embarrassed and ashamed, which only made the symptoms worse.

Once I finally learned how to rebuild my inner safety and strengthen my serotonin system properly, the panic attacks disappeared.

When the sympathetic nervous system's 'fight' response is activated, you may feel angry and frustrated more easily, like someone has wronged you. Life looks black and white, and you can become defensive. Compromising becomes hard and anxiety and restlessness fill our bodies. You might feel like someone is after you or you are continuously two steps behind. If you are unable to relax, you may open your laptop outside of work hours to check your email 'just in case'.

Ready to fight or run away from the threat, your muscles tense up and your breathing becomes shallow. Your heart rate rises and your sweat glands activate. Your eyes may feel dry and the muscles behind the eyes become strained. These are all bodily responses to the activation of the sympathetic nervous system or, as it can also be called, the stress response.

Open your vision

When we are stressed, the brain is focused on locating the source of threat and our vision becomes narrower. Make a conscious effort to broaden your vision by looking at nature, a large painting, a theatre stage or a movie screen. You can even just move your eyes from side to side. By consciously broadening our visual focus, we signal to our nervous system that everything is okay, triggering the relaxation response in the body and helping our nervous system to calm down and the stress levels to decrease.

For our ancestors, the main causes of stress were mostly related to uncertainty around survival: gathering enough food, having shelter and enough clean water to drink, as well as social dynamics – or of course the potential risk of a sabre-toothed tiger attacking you. For many of us in the privileged West today, our need for more safety is activated by both everyday life stresses and a deeper layer of subconscious stress. A tight deadline at work, the worry and strain of taking care of elderly parents, not getting your needs met in your relationships, carrying old emotions in your body or working in a job that is not aligned with your values can all be sources of threat to your nervous system. You get an email from your boss that makes your heart skip a beat. Someone drives too slowly in front of you and you honk and wave your fist, cursing how idiots like that are even allowed to drive. For the nervous system, it doesn't matter if the cause of the stress is an email from your boss or a sabre-toothed tiger jumping from a bush – it activates the stress response.

We can't think ourselves into safety. We can't overanalyse or convince ourselves that everything is fine. The only way to calm down a strained nervous system is to help the body feel safe again.

We can use different ways to signal safety to our bodies and help balance the serotonin system. It can be movement, touch or even using your voice to activate the vagus nerve and calm down the stress response. On my own journey, it was meditation that helped me to take a pause so that I could finally see clearly. After darkness, meditation felt like someone had turned on the light. I could see the wood from the trees and which steps to take to find the safety within.

Before we look at the power of meditation and other tools to regulate the nervous system, it's worth noting that, if you've been living with an imbalanced serotonin system or an overactive nervous system, you might have resistance to the idea of meditating and pausing. If high dopamine and high cortisol states have been your 'normal' for a long time, your brain will seek safety from these behaviours.

Your brain is a predictive machine in charge of orchestrating every bodily function. It relies on energy flow and information from both within and outside the body to predict how we should use our energy. Is it safe enough to heal? Or do we need to restore energy for future needs? Based on what has happened in the past, your brain predicts the future and prepares your body to have the necessary energy to act accordingly: to fight, run away or collapse.

Starting a new practice that lowers your stress levels, such as meditation, yoga or stretching, can be a warning signal for the body. If you have trained your brain to expect continuous high stress levels, you can develop a sense of comfort by being surrounded by conflicts, hurry and drama.

When calmness threatens your body, you might feel uneasy when things slow down at work or if there are no fires that you need to put out. You may dive into family dynamics and look for things that need fixing. Having a quiet Sunday morning without the kids can feel like a relaxing idea, but soon, you might notice worrying thoughts flooding your mind, and you just need to start doing something! This is your brain trying to keep you safe.

To ease the slowly rising feeling of dis-ease with the lower-than-normal stress hormones, you might start looking for a fight, or go to that one social media account that always irritates you. When calm doesn't feel safe, we tend to create familiar situations to behave in a way we always have. We need to get our daily dose of stress hormones, and our mind will find them – if we let it!

And so a loop is created. When we are addicted to our own stress hormones, we seek safety from the comfort of the known dramas and the familiar messes. And as low stress hormone levels are a sign of danger to the body, we are pulled by high-stress situations or create them ourselves. This strengthens these neural pathways in our brain, making pausing feel even more dangerous for the body. But thankfully, our brains are malleable and we can learn to pause and reset our serotonin system.

> Boredom and anxiety are both our attempts to avoid unpleasant emotional states. When we are addicted to stress hormones, we get easily bored and anxious in order to stay in the familiar level of stress.

As we've seen, the brain is a habit machine, trying to save energy wherever possible and choosing the most used pathways. Thoughts, beliefs, behavioural patterns – the brain always chooses the easiest route. This is why letting go of old ways of being requires an active pause: we need energy to create new neural pathways. But every time we decide to behave a different way, the new synaptic connections strengthen. And this new version of yourself soon starts feeling more familiar.

Over to you

- Do you feel easily anxious or bored?
- Do you lose your temper often?
- Are you drawn to high-stress situations?
- Were you surrounded by drama or uncertainty when you were growing up?
- Do you feel like meditation is not for you?

Meditation: Turning on the light

When we meditate, the energy waves in our brains change: they go from intense and sharp gamma waves to low-flowing alpha and theta waves. Gamma waves are linked to high-alert states, such as active problem-solving and intense concentration. With gamma waves, you can think of intense spikes of energy going up and down that keep your mind busy and blabbering. Alpha and theta waves are slower and more relaxed – the energy is the same, but the waves go out longer and the energy expands. In theta state, the transverse neurons in our brains can rest and we switch on creativity and problem-solving. We have the capacity to see the bigger picture again, and the image that we see is no longer coloured by fear.

After meditation or a body scan, your mind may feel like it has more space. It's as if you can see the wood from the trees. This is because meditation soothes the wired-up amygdala (the fear centre) in your brain and lowers your stress hormone levels. When your amygdala is no longer overactive, like a guard dog ready to bark at anyone who sets their feet close to the premises, your brain no longer fixates on only finding signs of danger from the environment. Your mind relaxes, and so does your body.

When your parasympathetic nervous system activates, and you are in a rest-and-digest response, your mind finally has the bandwidth to come up with new ideas and create new solutions. You have the space to see new possibilities. Your thinking is no longer based on fear and the lights are on.

So, how do you meditate?

1. Begin by finding a quiet space where you can sit comfortably. This can be on a pillow, on the sofa or on the floor.
2. Set a manageable time limit, especially if you are new to meditation, perhaps starting with just 5–10 minutes.
3. Sit with your back straight, and close your eyes if you feel comfortable doing so.
4. Direct your attention to your breath, focusing on the sensation of each inhale and exhale.
5. As you breathe, thoughts may arise. Acknowledge them without judgement and gently guide your focus back to your breath. Some people find it helpful to use a mantra, a repeated word or phrase, to maintain focus:

   • 'So Hum' ('I am that') is a simple mantra that focuses on the breath and has been shown to induce a meditative state by synchronising brain waves.
   • 'I am' is a simple affirmation that increases self-esteem, self-acceptance and feelings of personal power.
   • Repeating the mantra 'Let go' can help reduce stress and facilitate acceptance of difficult situations.

If observing your thoughts is hard, you can try the following exercise.

1. Imagine driving a car on a motorway, looking out of the window.
2. Visualise yourself stopping, then slowly stepping outside the car and climbing onto a hill next to the road.
3. From there, you can peacefully watch the cars passing by. Each car represents a thought.
4. If a thought grasps your attention and you find yourself driving the car again, you can always breathe in and move back to the hill to observe the colourful fleet of vehicles passing by.

Alternatively, you can explore meditation through a body scan, gradually bringing awareness to different parts of your body. Think of it as taking your focus off your thoughts, being curious and paying attention to the sensations in your body. How do your arms feel? Can you feel sensations in your stomach? Do you notice your heart beating? Scan through your whole body – from head to toe – bringing awareness to each part.

Adding even small moments of mindful awareness into your days can help calm your brain, body and mind. What colour mug would you like to choose for your tea this morning? Can you feel the warmth of the mug in your fingers? How does it feel as the warm liquid moves from your mouth to your throat and stomach?

Meditation is a great practice to have in your toolbox to calm down an overactive nervous system. However, it's not the only one. If you have lived in high-stress situations for a long time, pausing can feel dangerous to your brain. This is when you can use movement to create more safety and clarity.

Use your body to calm your mind

Our minds and bodies are two sides of the same coin – the neuroscientist Candace Pert, PhD, famously wrote: 'Your body is your subconscious mind' in her book of the same name. Our bodies tell the stories of our subconscious. When you feel attacked, your arms rise instinctively in order to protect yourself. You close your hands into fists in readiness to hit and attack. Your shoulders collapse, and you protect your stomach in the wake of an impending doom. What happens in the body also happens in the mind, and vice versa. When you know how to calm down your body, you are more able to pacify a fearful and panicky mind in the moment – and gradually have more energy and clarity to take the next step.

As I've mentioned, for years I suffered from crippling back pain. I remember lying in an MRI machine in my local A&E, listening to the machine's hollow metallic clanging. I had back pain so severe that I couldn't move from the floor. At that time, I didn't know that pain was a message that my body was feeling unsafe – the pain was my nervous system trying to tell me to get the hell of that toxic relationship that felt so familiar.

Peter A. Levine, a prominent figure in the field of trauma therapy and the developer of Somatic Experiencing, emphasises the body's physiological responses to stress and trauma. When we feel stressed and unsafe, the sympathetic nervous system activates and the stress hormones adrenaline and cortisol prepare our body for taking action. This can lead to the activation or engagement of various muscle groups, including the hip flexors, lower back and pelvic floor muscles, as the body braces itself for action or adopts defensive postures. Tension, after all, is a precursor to movement. However, if the stress becomes chronic and we stay in situations where our needs are not met, the muscles stay contracted and the tension and survival energy can get trapped.

You may suffer from continuous back pain that has no evident cause. Reflecting on my own experiences, repressed anger was most likely a key factor behind the intense back pain I endured, which seemed to appear out of nowhere and left doctors at a loss for solutions. The chronic tension kept my muscles contracted and trapped survival energy, resulting in ongoing pain. When we start viewing pain as a messenger, it can guide us toward finding more safety and balance in our lives. It may prompt us to have difficult conversations, set boundaries, prioritise rest, or even release the pain through actions like shaking or screaming, allowing energy to flow freely once more.

> Feel it to heal it. In order to heal we have to stop escaping pain and our feelings.

When the body perceives a threat, tiny, often unnoticed micro-movements such as muscle tensing, quickened breathing and pupil dilation, can prepare us for a flight-or-fight response. However, these same micro-movements can also be leveraged to induce a relaxation response.

To use micro-movements for relaxation, focus on consciously releasing muscle tension with movement like gently opening your palms, swaying from side to side or thumping your feet on the ground. You can also slow and deepen your breathing, constrict your pupils, soften your fingers, relax your jaw and release tension in your neck and shoulders. By mindfully attending to these subtle bodily cues and using movement to help the body to complete the stress cycle, you can signal to your nervous system that it's safe to enter a state of calm and rest. The posture of your body also reflects the state of your nervous system and whether or not you feel safe and connected. Throughout our lives our bodies have learned how to keep us safe and maximise opportunities for care and affection from our caregivers. All these stories are present in the way we move and hold our bodies. Sometimes freedom comes from teaching the body a new way to be yourself.

Psychotherapist and the mother of somatic psychotherapy, Pat Ogden, describes beautifully how our bodies' wisdom can be a route to self-discovery and freedom. Your mind can tell you that you are finally ready to leave your past behind you, but your body tells you that it's not finished. There is still tension to be released.

Our habitual memory is recorded in our postures and gestures. These habits of responding and moving in the world are carved deep into our psyche. We learn how to carry ourselves and how to move. We learn the ways we need to be in order to feel accepted and loved.

If you grew up with parents who valued high achievement and encouraged you to continuously try harder, your posture may reflect this influence. You might develop a feeling that you are not loved for who you are, but for what you do. And, as a result, your body might learn to be continuously tight, always ready to try harder and work harder – chin up high with determination. When we think about this posture from an energetic perspective, everything is stagnant. When the chest is held up high and the stomach is tucked in, the diaphragm can't move and the breath becomes shallow. The inability to move can then keep the sympathetic nervous system constantly active and the brain focusing on signs of danger and threat. As a result, the chest slowly loses its ability to move and the shoulders are constantly tight, unable to fully let go and relax. On a more spiritual level, the heart loses its softness and you may lose your ability to connect with others. The body is preparing for a world where anything can happen at any time.

Instead of listening to your body's messages and resting, you override the messages and continue doing, even though you are mentally or emotionally on the verge of burnout. This continual activation of the sympathetic nervous system can make it hard for you to properly recover and recharge your energy. And in the long run, it will start to show through different kind of symptoms. These procedurally learned postures, movements and tension patterns in your body can prevent you from taking chances and going after your dreams.

On the other hand, if you grew up in an environment where trying hard was discouraged, or everything you achieved was undervalued, ignored or dismissed, you might instead develop a sunken chest, limp arms and shallow breath. Your body will reflect the experience of not feeling confident and giving up. As an adult, these patterns may make it hard to mobilise the needed energy to complete a difficult task. Or maybe you don't even take the chance and try.

Your body holds tight to its energetic patterns that have given it safety in the past. However, these patterns don't always serve us in the present and they can become maps to where we still carry pain. You can help the body release stuck energy and aid micro-movements towards completion with the following somatic practices.

Shaking

Intentional shaking is a great way to release built-up tension and energy in the body and help balance the nervous system. This can help reduce stress, lower heart rate and blood pressure, and promote a state of calm and relaxation.

Below are some tips on how to shake to release emotional tension and stress:

- Find a private, comfortable space where you can move freely without distraction.
- Stand with your feet shoulder-width apart, knees slightly bent. Allow your arms to hang loosely at your sides.
- Take a few deep breaths to centre yourself. As you exhale, begin to shake your body gently. Start with small movements in your hands and arms, then gradually allow the shaking to move through your entire body.
- Don't try to control the shaking – let it flow naturally. Allow your body to move in whatever way feels right, without judgement.
- As you shake, focus on releasing any emotions, tension or stress you're holding on to. Imagine the shaking helping to dislodge and move that energy out of your body.

- Continue shaking for 5–10 minutes, or until you feel a release or sense of calm come over you.
- When finished, take a few more deep breaths and gently settle back into stillness. Notice how you feel in your body and emotions.

The key is to let the shaking be loose and unbridled, without overthinking it. This can be a very cathartic way to process and release pent-up feelings. Start slowly and be gentle with yourself. Over time, you may find the shaking becomes more natural and effective.

Shaking can also be used before a meditative practice, allowing the mind and body to settle into focused attention and present-moment awareness easily. You can try it any time – just put on your favourite song and start shaking your limbs and body. You might be surprised how well it works!

If shaking feels too strange for you, you can try doing some jumps or any muscle work or exercise that feels good for you before settling down to meditate.

TRE (Tension and Trauma Releasing Exercises)

Shaking and trembling is the body's natural way of releasing excess energy and bringing the nervous system back to balance. Trembling often happens naturally after a stressful event. Even animals in the wild shake and tremble to release excess energy. Letting the body run its course or even increasing the shaking intentionally can be a powerful tool on your journey. TRE is a therapeutic technique that can help the body release physical tension and emotional trauma through gentle exercises that naturally induce therapeutic tremors or shaking.

Wall push

The wall push is an exercise that can help release anger, frustration and sadness from the body:

- First, find a sturdy wall that can take the weight of your body.
- Place the palms of your hands against the wall and start pushing with all your power into the wall as if you are trying to move it.
- You can keep pushing until your arms, legs or core start to shake or shiver.
- This means that the energy meant to fuel your muscles to turn your fist and fight or run away from the situation as fast as possible is being discharged.
- You may also notice yourself crying. This is your nervous system's way of calming itself down and returning back to a sense of safety, supporting your serotonin levels.
- After you are done, take a break, breathe and check in with yourself. Can you still find anger or frustration in your body? Do you still have a feeling of sadness or being defeated? You can repeat the exercise as many times as needed.

When you stay at your desk instead of running and hiding after you get an upsetting email, you prevent the body from completing the intrinsic micro-movement that it was designed to go through when stressed. So, as all the survival energy has no outlet and stays inside you, the nervous system still believes the threat to be present. This simple exercise can help the energy flow through your body and communicate to your nervous system that the danger is over.

Rhythmic movement

Movements such as dancing, rocking and gentle swaying can also help us calm down and feel safe again by activating the vestibular system, which is linked to the ANS (autonomic nervous system). I still love to sway with my youngest child when my nervous system needs comfort or when I want to increase positive energy. This may be one of the reasons why dancing has been a sacred ritual in ancient cultures: dancing and movement can help you shift your state from fear to safety.

Breathing

Breathing is also a powerful tool to calm down the nervous system. When your nervous system is in fight-or-flight mode, your breathing becomes shallow as the body priori-tises sending oxygen into the muscles as much and as fast as possible. As a result, the diaphragm, the primary muscle responsible for your breathing, contracts but is unable to relax fully during exhalation and your breathing becomes shallow.

Shallow breathing is also a sign of danger to the nervous system. When you are stressed and your sympathetic nervous system is activated, your breathing becomes shallow as a result. And because shallow breathing signals danger to the nervous system, the inability to breathe in fully can keep your body in the fight-or-flight response. Therefore, if you want to end the cycle of fear and create more space, breathing is one of the easiest ways to shift your nervous system state from fear to safety.

One of my favourite breathing exercises is the 4 x 4, or box breathing, as it is also called. This breathing exercise can be a fast way to calm down your nervous system and reduce stress.

- Start by inhaling through your nose and counting to four. As you breathe in, use your finger to draw the first side of an imaginary box into the air.
- Then hold your breath and count to four, drawing the next side of the box in the air.
- Breathe out and count to four again as you draw the third side of the box in front of you.
- Hold your breath, count to four, and draw the last side of the box.
- Repeat this three times and notice how you feel.

Do you sense more space in your mind? Do you notice more softness in your body?

'Be' with your emotions

In his book *In an Unspoken Voice*, Peter A. Levine describes how emotions can get stuck in our bodies if we don't allow them to move through us. And as emotions are energy in motion, if that energy is stuck in the body, it also stagnates our mind into loops. Your mind is replaying a fight with your boss over and over again. You find yourself thinking about nasty comments, even weeks after the incident is over. You continue to feel worried – only the reason seems to change. There is an uncomfortable feeling of general anxiety, always preparing for the worst. This is because your brain is trying to find a reason for your internal state.

All the emotions that stay trapped in the body can be seen as armour that the body holds to protect itself. The armour is built of bodily expressions that have been suppressed or held back. So, instead of tension being released through expression, the tension stays in the body. The gateway to change is noticing what emotions feel familiar to you – and consciously changing these patterns. You can you teach your body and redefine what emotions feel familiar to it. When you release the trapped energy, you free up space and give the emotions a route to express themselves.

You can release these tension patterns through different hands-on therapeutic methods, such as massage or osteopathy. But as long as the root cause is not addressed and you stay in a situation that is causing you strain, the same behavioural patterns, such as overpleasing or not expressing your needs and emotions, such as frustration, anger or sadness, are likely going to manifest in your body as tension again.

The next time you feel angry or sad after yoga or a somatic practice, be with the emotion and feel it. Pay attention to the physical sensations, thoughts and behaviours associated with the emotion. Recognise that it's okay to feel whatever you're feeling, without trying to change or suppress it. Accept the emotion without judgement or criticism. You can remind yourself that it's okay to feel vulnerable or uncomfortable at times, and that experiencing emotions is a normal and healthy part of life. You can also use movement to help you stay present with the emotion. Allow the emotion to naturally rise and fall. Trust that emotions, like waves, come and go in their own time. Letting go of attachment to the emotion can help you move through it with greater ease and grace.

When you hold your attention simultaneously on the physical sensations and other aspects of the experience, such as balance or your thoughts, you create dual awareness. With dual awareness you strengthen your capacity to be with difficult emotions – and let them flow through you. Dual awareness not only helps your nervous system to relax – and therefore strengthens your serotonin system – but it can help the brain to process difficult emotions and make sense of memories that are arising from the body. By fostering greater integration of mind and body, dual awareness practices can facilitate healing, transformation and the cultivation of embodied well-being.

Being with and accepting intense bodily sensations such as pain is hard, though. I remember lying on the floor, unable to move with my back pain, with the fear and despair that *this is it: I have lost my health*. The horror of being stuck with the pain and never gaining back my health affected my sleep and a negative spiral began: I couldn't sleep because of the pain, and because of the lack of sleep, the pain got worse. The anxiety of not knowing when the pain would next strike and who would be there to help me to work with it was limiting me in everything I did. I needed to know that there was always an osteopath or a chiropractor near all the places I went. I was, in a sense, addicted to knowing that someone else could always help me and make me feel better.

When I learned to increase my trust in my own capacity to heal myself, my pain eased. With every step, serotonin was showing me the way back to myself – and trusting that I did have the strength to have my own back.

When you learn how to teach your brain and body to feel safer, you can feel more balanced and relaxed. However, the experiences of the generations before us also affect how our bodies react to different situations. Sometimes the pain we carry is not even ours, but it, too, can be unpacked and healed.

How Trauma Can Shake
Your Serotonin System

Trauma is translated from Greek, and it means 'wound' – a wound in our psyche, a pain that reaches all the way to our soul. Trauma can be the horrors of war tearing our very humanity apart. Or it can even be a seemingly benign event that leaves us feeling trapped in terror.

In order to understand how trauma can shake the serotonin system, it's important for us to clarify first what we mean when we use the word 'trauma'. Trauma is our emotional response to an event that we don't have the means to cope with. Trauma can include serious illnesses, witnessing violence, racism, abandonment, bullying, getting into an accident, mental or physical abuse or assault. Sometimes a surgery or a medical procedure can lead to trauma. Or a feeling of not being seen and heard as a child or getting really frightened by something. The essence of trauma is that the event shatters your sense of safety to the core, leaving you with overwhelming fear – and a helpless sense that there is nothing you can do to escape the situation.

Experiencing a traumatic event can shake the foundations of the serotonin system: it can diminish a person's sense of safety, blur their sense of self and shrink the ability to regulate emotions and navigate through relationships. Trauma can leave us feeling paralysed and lost in this world. We freeze from fear and terror, leave our bodies and seek safety from inside our minds in the absence of an empathic other who would hold space for us to feel safe when experiencing the overwhelming thoughts, feelings and emotions of the situation.

Trauma can affect your serotonin system in multiple ways:

- Trauma is not only in your head; it's something that happens in your body, leaving you scared stiff, overwhelmed or with a sense of defeat and helplessness. It's an emotional wound that also affects how our brain functions. Trauma can impair the brain's ability to adapt and form new neural connections (see page 75 for more on neuroplasticity) and how our brains develop and process information. When we release the subconscious stress, dissolve the traumatic memory and integrate it, we can support our brain's information processing and functioning, including the regulation of serotonin production.

- Trauma can keep people stuck in the past and prevent them living fully in the present moment. Unable to put the past into rest, traumatised people often keep reliving the traumatic experience over and over again. Our bodies can often use immense energy to keep the painful memories and emotions under control. This continuous subconscious stress (from suppressing emotions instead of acknowledging and feeling them) and the prolonged release of cortisol, adrenaline and other stress hormones can prevent the serotonin system from working properly.

- Trauma can lead to chronic inflammation, negatively impacting serotonin synthesis and metabolism. As the trauma is successfully addressed and dissolved, inflammation levels tend to decrease, allowing for better serotonin functioning.

- The gut is extremely sensitive to the chronic emotional and subconscious stress caused by trauma. For example, chronic constipation and low-grade inflammation in the gut can be effects of trauma showing up in our bodies and affecting the serotonin levels as a significant portion of serotonin is produced in the gut.

- Trauma can also be behind many auto-immune diseases, such as diabetes, rheumatoid arthritis, asthma, psoriasis and Crohn's disease. Healing trauma can help to lower the cortisol and adrenaline levels in the body, contributing to a stronger serotonin system.

We all carry wounds, but not all of them are ours. Some of our pain is inherited from the generations before us.

Working through the pain that travels through generations

The basis of our serotonin system and our sense of safety develops in the first moments of life. In the womb, we learn what the world is like from the hormones we are immersed in. We may not have complete form yet or understand words or languages, but, since our first moments, our bodies understand the language of our mother's hormones.

In every step, we carry the pain from our ancestors in our bodies – the beliefs that make us curl up and protect ourselves; the feeling of never being good enough. 'We are all museums of fear', as poet Charles Bukowski wisely wrote. But if we want to break free and explore the world with both our wings and hearts open, we need to break the cycle of pain and start the healing.

I never met my grandfather, as he died when my mother was only in her twenties. I've heard, though, that my grandfather was a very intelligent and generous man. He had built successful businesses and a beautiful family, but the war had left its mark on him. He medicated the pain and traumatic events of war by drinking. And when he drank, he changed completely. He would lock my grandmother and their three kids in the cellar and shoot around the house with his gun. In my toxic relationship, during one of our fights, my partner locked me in a room. There in that room, I came to a sudden realisation that maybe I was living through and acting out this transgenerational trauma; the trauma coming back from previous generations. Maybe I had to come this far to be able to heal it.

The research on epigenetics shows how traumatic events, such as war or famine, can leave a mark on us at a genetic level. In their book *Super Genes*, Dr Deepak Chopra and Dr Rudolph E. Tanzi build a case for how our inner and outer environment can change our gene expression without changing the DNA sequence itself through changed DNA methylation patterns. DNA methylation is a process that determines how genes are read and expressed. You can think of the methylation process as our bodies' way of leaving tags on different parts of DNA that either turn them on or off.

The environments we live in and the experiences we have can leave an epigenetic mark on us and affect how our genes express themselves. We then pass these epigenetic changes on to future generations.

A groundbreaking study by Brian G. Dias and Kerry J. Ressler published in the prestigious *Nature* magazine in 2014 reveals that traumatic experiences can cause epigenetic changes that are passed down to future generations, that affect how they behave. In the study, the researchers conditioned male rats to fear a cherry blossom scent (acetophenone) by pairing it with mild shocks to their feet. Soon, the rats learned to associate the cherry blossom scent with the electric shocks and became afraid of the scent.

The offspring of these conditioned rats, as well as the subsequent generation, were found to have an increased sensitivity to the cherry blossom scent, despite never having been exposed to the scent of cherry blossoms before themselves or experiencing the associated shocks.

The researchers discovered that the sperm of the conditioned rats showed epigenetic changes, specifically alterations in DNA methylation patterns to the gene that is responsible for encoding the receptor that detects the cherry blossom scent. As a result, the brains of the offspring had more neurons that were responsive to the cherry blossom scent, indicating that the changes in behaviour were linked to structural changes in the brain, likely driven by the epigenetic modifications inherited from the parents.

The good news is that we can also pass down healing. When we heal old fears and teach our nervous system to react to different stimulus in a new way, our children and grandchildren can also inherit our healing.

Signs your body might be holding on to an unresolved trauma

- Chronic pain and tension
- Exhaustion and difficulty sleeping
- Digestive issues
- Feeling numb and dissociated
- Unexplained physical symptoms
- Weakened immune system
- Lack of emotional control

Due to trauma and pain, our bodies can hold on to the past and prevent us from living fully in the now. But when we bring our pain into the light and do the inner work, we can heal the pain, even from generations ago.

You don't need to know *what* happened or *why* you seek safety by behaving in specific ways. Trauma doesn't speak in words; it speaks through our bodies.

For trauma and deep pain, I've seen excellent results with Eye Movement Desensitisation and Reprocessing (EMDR). It was also a life-saving practice when I needed help in letting go of disturbing images and sensations from my traumatic relationship. EMDR was one of the tools that helped my body let go of the past and live in the now.

EMDR can be a great way to treat trauma and PTSD (Post Traumatic Stress Disorder). With the help of rapid eye movements, sounds and tapping, the method can help people process and integrate traumatic memories, as well as let go of negative beliefs and replace them with positive, more empowering ones.

EMDR can be an effective tool to help let go of mental images and disturbing bodily sensations and start living anew – not dragging the past with you anymore. Though EMDR can technically be done on oneself, because of the intense emotions it can bring up, it's recommended to do it under the guidance of a trained professional. However, with other milder wounds and traumas, you can use some of the techniques introduced in the next two chapters. First, let's look at a simple way of communicating safety to the nervous system – with 'glimmers'.

Look out for the glimmers

Deb Dana is a clinician and consultant specialising in polyvagal theory and working with complex trauma. She coined the term 'glimmers', which are tiny moments of awe, sparking joy and calm in your body system. When we intentionally learn how to shift our focus to glimmers throughout the day, we increase positive energy flow in the body. Feelings of ease, joy, awe and gratitude start feeling more familiar to you – and soon, your brain chooses these pathways over others. Glimmers reduce emotional distress and can help us be more in the learning zone from where it's also easier to do the trauma/inner work.

Glimmers could be mindfully noticing how the warmth of the sun feels on your face or how loving words from a friend make you feel inside. Glimmers might be taking note of how you feel when you cuddle with your pet or paying attention to how time alone in the morning or listening to music feels in your body. Learning how to focus on the good and the energising can strengthen the nervous system and increase your sense of well-being and energy.

Think of changing the wiring in your brain like driving on

a foggy evening. Imagine driving a car and coming to a cross-roads, consciously pressing the brake and slowing down before choosing which way to turn. On the right, you see there is an outcome that you are ready to let go. It can be having too little money in your bank account, always having too much work or not having time to exercise, just to mention a few. On the left you can see a sunny, clear sky. You feel more at peace. You have the energy and time to invest in yourself. You feel happy and at ease.

Every time you pause before making a decision, you have the possibility to choose differently. Every time you decide differently, you start making new pathways that take you to the life on the left-hand side. The more often you choose to pause and turn left, the more momentum this movement gains – and soon, the car turns there more easily and you start consciously making decisions that support the future you want to build.

If you want to increase your ability to feel more confident, safe and relaxed, you have to build your capacity for those emotions. When an emotion doesn't feel familiar to your body, it's important to play with the capacity that you have for that emotion at this moment. You don't need to feel 100 per cent safe or confident for the emotion to be present. When you turn your focus inwards, can you gauge a percentage of how, let's say, relaxed your body feels now? Is there even a small part of you that feels confident? Can you find that part in your body, place your hand on it and be with it?

> Remember you are not healing to be able to handle trauma; you are used to trauma. You are healing so you can handle ease and joy.

Therapeutic methods and practices for working with transgenerational trauma

Here are some practices that can be helpful on your healing journey. There is a lot we can do ourselves when we take a deep and honest look within and start recognising the family patterns and experiences that can run deep in our bodies and minds. However, we are built *from* connection *for* connection – this is why working with a trusted professional is integral to looking at the psychic wounds that trauma can create so we can successfully heal the pain.

- **Genogram work:** Where you create a visual family tree to illuminate family dynamics, relationship patterns and areas of trauma across the generations.
- **Ancestral healing:** Involves exploring family history, conducting ancestral rituals and engaging in guided meditations to connect with and heal ancestral lineages.
- **Emotional Freedom Techniques (EFT):** Also known as 'tapping', EFT is a self-guided technique that uses acupressure points to release emotional blockages and traumas (we will cover this in Chapter 8).
- **Somatic therapy:** Focuses on the connection between the body, emotions and the nervous system to process and release trauma. Includes techniques like Somatic Experiencing, Psychophysical Physiotherapy, Primitive Reflex Therapy and Sensorimotor Psychotherapy.

- **Family systems therapy:** Examines the dynamics and patterns within the family unit to address transgenerational issues. Includes approaches like Family Constellations and Internal Family Systems Therapy (IFS). IFS Therapy falls under the broader umbrella of family systems therapies and takes a unique approach by focusing on the internal 'family' of 'parts' within us. IFS explores how these internal parts interact and seeks to bring harmony.
- **Integrative therapy:** Combines healing modalities, such as psychotherapy, bodywork and mindfulness practices. Requires the expertise of a licensed mental health professional to provide a comprehensive treatment plan.

When we find ways to heal our pain, we actually work with the pain that has been carried in our bodies for generations.

The power of intuition

Intuition is a profound source of inner wisdom. It's an innate knowing that transcends logical reasoning, often guiding us towards choices and paths that align with our deeper desires and purpose. By tapping into our intuition, we gain access to a wellspring of wisdom that can lead to greater fulfilment, authenticity and growth.

However, unresolved wounds and traumas can obstruct the journey of listening to our intuition.

Traumatic experiences, whether recent or from our past, can create internal imbalances, distort our perception and cloud the clarity of our intuition. Unresolved trauma may manifest as negative beliefs, self-doubt, fear or emotional triggers that interfere with our ability to discern our true intuition from the lingering echoes of pain.

As you work through your wounds and traumas, you create space for intuition to flourish. Integration occurs when the wounds are acknowledged, healed and transformed, allowing your intuition to become a guiding force in your life.

By listening to your intuition from a place of wholeness, you can navigate decisions, relationships and life choices with greater clarity and alignment. Trust in the wisdom that emerges from within, understanding that your intuition is a powerful compass, guiding you towards authentic expression, personal growth and a life of purpose.

We've seen how trauma and unconscious fears can disrupt the serotonin system, leading to distressing physical and mental symptoms. You've learned some practical techniques to calm the nervous system and rebuild healthy serotonin levels. By addressing the root causes, you can regain control over your mind and body.

In the next chapter, we'll explore how building healthy boundaries is another highly effective way to strengthen your serotonin system in the long term.

Chapter 7

Building Healthy Boundaries

When you don't have clear and strong boundaries, your energy begins to leak into other people and the environment around you. Without even noticing, you give too much away and, with nothing left for yourself, you are depleted. You may start to feel bitter and frustrated, angry and irritable. Maybe you have an uneasy sense that people are using you or taking you for granted. Your connection to your personal needs grows brittle, so when someone asks how you are, you either dismiss it with untruths ('just amazing!') or you feel low and empty (and don't really know why). You lose yourself to the perceived needs of others. This chapter is all about how you can firm up your protections around your energy and resources, so that you build yourself up to your best capacity.

Maintaining healthy boundaries is not just about protecting ourselves, though; it's a vital component in regulating our serotonin levels. By establishing clear limits and learning to prioritise our needs, we can significantly reduce the chronic stress that, as we saw in the last chapter, can disrupt serotonin production. This, in turn, fosters improved self-regulation and a sense of safety and control, creating stronger and more fulfilling relationships.

How healthy boundaries can influence serotonin

- Healthy boundaries help reduce chronic subconscious stress and the associated release of cortisol, which can disrupt serotonin production. It can be easy to think that there is no harm in saying 'yes' just this one time. However, your nervous system knows when you are doing things only to please others or from a fear of being judged. Learning to recognise whether you are making decisions based on old fears or from a state of standing firmly on your own two feet is important to your serotonin system. By tuning into your own needs, setting clear limits and learning to say 'no' when necessary, you can better manage your stress levels, allowing serotonin levels to stabilise.

- Healthy boundaries are also an important factor in creating a sense of safety and control over one's environment and relationships. This feeling of safety and control can have a calming effect on the nervous system, promoting the release of serotonin and therefore increasing our sense of peace and safety.

- Serotonin is linked to our mood and sense of self-worth. Healthy boundaries can enhance self-esteem and confidence as you learn to prioritise your needs and advocate for yourself. This can help to create a balanced serotonin system.

- Healthy boundaries in life lead to more respectful, authentic and fulfilling connections. When we have the courage to show up as who we are and express our needs, we no longer have to sacrifice ourselves in order to fit into other people's demands. We are built for both authenticity and connection – and our serotonin system needs us to feel safe and accepted just as we are in our relationships.

In my early relationships, my boundaries had been violated and crushed on every level. I felt as if life had been sucked away from me. With support from my friends and family and the clarity gained from meditation, which we explored in the previous chapter, I found the strength to leave. However, when I looked back at my childhood, I noticed that I hadn't learned how to build boundaries around myself. It was time to learn how to break the cycle.

I remember growing up without having any real privacy. My mother was a fiercely loving person who cared for us with her every cell and did everything for us. Maybe due to her own anxieties, she would also read my diaries and enter my room without knocking. There was nothing just for me – everything seemed to be public.

This sense of merging together and not having clear boundaries between me and my family continued into adulthood. I would feel guilty if I didn't ask my mother and father to join us at my summer cottage. I would walk over eggshells to ensure that everyone was happy. We were one unit, taking responsibility for each other's feelings.

The lack of boundaries has shown up later in my life as oversharing and letting people both in business and my private life get very close to me – maybe even too close at times. Both are things that I am still working on.

If you grew up in a family with loose or no boundaries, you might find it very difficult to say 'no'. You may find it hard to voice your true needs or ask for what you need. For example, instead of asking for a healthy fee for your professional services, you may find yourself giving out your time and expertise for free. Instead of asking for help, you take care of the entire household and the children, feeling exhausted and bitter. You might appease constantly and keep everyone else happy, only to find yourself exhausted. You have the tendency to jump into relationships where there is someone who needs to be saved. And if you are in a relationship, even a bad one, where you strongly feel the other person would not survive without you, you stay – even if the relationship keeps eating you from the inside out.

When you don't have clear boundaries, it can be hard to see yourself, and you will constantly be asking for validation from the world around you. Am I making my parents proud? Does everybody at work see how irreplaceable I am? Do my Instagram friends see how great I am doing? And if someone doesn't give it to you, it hurts. You feel alive only in the praising gaze of other people. When you can't really see yourself, you need to be seen by others.

When you start working on your boundaries, often the first people who resist this change are those who benefit from the situation and your weak boundaries. Surround yourself with people who support you in creating new boundaries. Talking with a trusted friend or having a therapist by your side can help the process. It will take time, but trust me, it will get easier and start to pay back!

The other side of the coin is to be someone who has boundaries that are incredibly strong, but that are not protecting you in the right way. You may build a rock-solid fence around your heart when something in the past has scared you or hurt too much. You can't imagine going through the pain again, so you don't allow life to flow in. You don't really let people in and if you do, you are sceptical, scrutinising the other person and continuously monitoring them for a mistake, a red flag that they, too, will hurt you. As a result, you isolate yourself and feel alone, even when surrounded by people. You won't let anyone hurt you again at any cost, but the price you pay is a deep sense of disconnection and loneliness.

However, we as human beings were built for connection. We ache to be seen, heard and loved for who we truly are. This false feeling of security, which comes from having unbreakably strict boundaries and not allowing people to connect with you, will stop you from evolving, from loving and from healing. We need other people to work through our pain. We must learn how to trust again if we want to heal.

When your boundaries aren't strong enough or aren't serving you, you can imagine how your energy leaks. Healthy boundaries help us protect our energy and keep us safe.

Over to you

- Do you often feel drained or depleted after spending time with certain people or in particular situations – but still feel like you have to?

- Do you have a hard time saying 'no' to requests or demands from others, even when they conflict with your own needs and priorities?
- Do you rarely share your true feelings and opinions with the people in your life, fearing their reaction or judgement?
- Do you tend to isolate yourself or shut people out to protect yourself?
- Have you built such strong emotional barriers that it's difficult for you to be vulnerable and authentic in your relationships?
- Do you constantly worry about what others think of you or seek their approval?
- Have you experienced a pattern of repeated boundary violations in your relationships yet struggled to set clearer limits?

Every 'Fuck This Shit' is an Opportunity

In boundary building, anger and rage are your friends, signalling to you to pause and ask yourself: *What is stepping on my boundaries and causing me strain? Are there areas in my life where my deepest needs are unmet?*

When you feel frustrated, afraid or offended, these emotions are your body's way of telling you that someone has stepped over your boundaries. They are energetic signs that something is no longer working for you, and this energy is preparing you for action.

Every time you feel jealous of someone on social media or are shouting 'fuck this shit!' into the void, it's your body telling you that there is a golden coin hidden in the mud. When you learn how to listen to feelings like anger, jealousy, hurt or frustration, you have an opportunity to heal something new – and become more whole in yourself.

Our emotions are powerful barometers of the state of our boundaries. When we pay attention to how we feel, we gain invaluable insight into where our boundaries may need to be adjusted or strengthened.

Anger, for example, is often a clear sign that a boundary has been crossed. Perhaps someone has asked too much of us, overlooked our needs or disrespected our limits. Rather than suppressing this anger, we can use it as a call to action – to stand up for ourselves and communicate our boundaries more firmly.

Conversely, chronic feelings of guilt or obligation point to blurred boundaries. We may be giving away too much of ourselves at the expense of our own well-being. Here, the antidote is learning to say 'no' without apology and reclaim your right to prioritise your own needs.

Anxiety can also indicate a boundary issue – either that we've allowed our boundaries to become too porous or that we've built them up as an impenetrable fortress. Anxiety reminds us to seek balance and to open ourselves up enough to connect authentically while still protecting our inner landscape.

Even positive emotions like joy and contentment can guide us. When we feel a sense of ease and fullness in our relationships and circumstances, it's often a sign that our boundaries function healthily – allowing the right amount of exchange and intimacy.

The key is to start tuning into our emotions' messages.

Rather than judging them or trying to make them disappear, we can approach them with curiosity, asking: *What is this feeling trying to tell me about my boundaries? How can I respond to this emotion in a way that honours and strengthens my sense of self?*

By using our emotions as boundary compasses, we cultivate a deeper self-awareness and the confidence to make the changes that allow us to show up more fully in our lives. Our feelings become allies in keeping our hearts soft and our boundaries strong.

'Who do you think you are, some fucking J. Lo?' was the reaction I got after I told an ex-boyfriend about my dream of combining science and entertainment, acting and being a doctor; having a career without boxes, where I could follow what sparks my joy – a career that was based on me expressing myself freely and sharing good to the world. Since I was a child, acting and entertainment has pulled me like a magnet. My big picture was starting to formulate. And there he was, trying to push me down with his words.

The words hurt me, but deep inside they fired me up; they brought me *sisu*. Sisu is a Finnish word, a concept that can be described as almost stoic determination, grit and bravery. Sisu is energy rising all the way up from your depths, a vigour to endure, a courage that grows when you know that you are taking action against the odds – but you still have the guts to move forward.

In my case, following my spark felt so profoundly intertwined with my very being that the idea of not pursuing it felt like fighting against my own nature. But instead of caging me down, his words made me lift my chin with a fiery determination. It was time to celebrate my inner J. Lo and bring her to life.

I learned to lean into my aggression in the arms of the deep green Finnish forests. After all that time of being put down and feeling hopeless and trapped, it was yelling in the woods that gave an outlet to all the anger in me. I yelled out my pain. I yelled out the disappointment of the relationship never being what I thought it had been. I yelled out the grief of letting go of an image of us that was never true – a future that never happened. In the secure comfort of the forest, little by little, I grew and learned how to own my aggression.

In those moments, maybe even for the first time, I was *with* my anger. I didn't try to mask it. I didn't run away from it. I was in my body and felt with my every cell how my boundaries had been violated. My muscles were ready to push any intruder away from my space. I felt the need for authentic expression stemming from the depths of my gut. And it felt good.

I was my own person, standing on my own ground. I was no longer meshed with another, not knowing where I ended and where someone else started. And because I had my own form and boundaries, I had the capacity to truly connect with others again. My boundaries gave me my voice back – and I learned how to connect with myself again.

In the past, I had often ignored or suppressed my emotions, viewing them as a weakness rather than a strength. However, as I began to pause and truly tune into how I was feeling, I discovered that my emotions were a powerful guide in helping me identify where my boundaries needed to be reinforced or recalibrated.

At first, the people who had grown accustomed to me having no boundaries resisted this new-found self-awareness. They would push back, try to make me feel guilty or even lash out when I began setting clearer limits. But I knew that honouring my emotions and my need for self-protection was essential, no matter how uncomfortable the process might be. If you recognise yourself in this, use the strategies below to create boundaries and build a shield of serotonin around you, protecting your energy.

Strategies for building stronger boundaries

- Express your boundary needs from a calm, centred state, not in the heat of an argument or intense emotion.
- Lean on the support of trusted friends and loved ones who can validate your boundary work and provide encouragement.
- Practise articulating your boundaries in a clear, confident way. It may feel awkward at first, but it gets easier with time.
- Remember that the people who have benefitted from your lack of boundaries will often oppose your boundary setting the most.
- Start by setting boundaries in easier, lower-stake situations before tackling more challenging relationships or circumstances.
- Remember that creating healthy boundaries is not about erecting walls – it's about striking the right balance between protecting yourself and being open to connection.
- Respect that others also have a right to their own boundaries, even if they differ from yours. Compromise is often part of boundary-setting in relationships.

The first time you enforce a boundary it might feel strange, alien, as if you're going against a lifetime of habits. The key is to connect with your gut feeling and build an awareness of what it feels like to act in a way that is true to you and protects your energies.

Every time you notice an energy leak it's like finding a spot where you can strengthen your energetic shield and support a sustainable flow of serotonin through your daily actions.

Be Gentle with Yourself

Setting up a boundary after your boundaries have been violated can feel highly unsafe for your nervous system. This is because often the bodily sensations of standing your ground, saying 'no' and potentially pissing someone off can be unfamiliar. Every emotion we carry and every experience we have creates a physical sensation in our bodies, and, as we touched on in the last chapter, the body feels comfortable with the emotions it experiences the most.

If you grew up in a demanding environment with a lot of stress, your body got used to experiencing these feelings from early on, so they feel familiar. Later in life, feeling overwhelmed can feel so familiar to you that you continue to place yourself in situations where you don't get what you need. You find yourself in one-sided friendships. You work in jobs where you can't express your true gifts. Your inner voice is harsh and critical, causing you to feel stressed. You want to feel more joy and ease, but your body doesn't really know how.

This is what psychologist Gay Hendricks refers to as the 'inner thermostat' in his bestselling book, *The Big Leap*. Our bodies have an imaginary thermostat setting and, because we automatically choose a familiar hell over an unfamiliar heaven, we self-sabotage when things are going too well. We start a fight with our spouse. We avoid doing the things we know are important to achieving our dreams. We create stressful situations and choose strain over joy and relaxation because being fulfilled and getting what we need doesn't feel familiar.

By doing this work on your boundaries, you are rewiring the amygdala (the fear centre) and creating new neural pathways so you are better able to handle more peace, calmness and joy – switching your serotonin to a more desirable setting.

When you shift your focus, even in the smallest of ways, a big change can happen. Little by little, you will have the capacity to operate more and more from that place – and modify your thermostat settings for the future. And after some time, the new heaven starts feeling more familiar than the old hell.

> Remember that growth can be uncomfortable. There will be a phase where your old self is gone, but the new self is still forming. It can be challenging, but trust the process and keep going – it will be worth it.

In the next chapter we'll look at the steps you can take to let go of limiting beliefs and rebuild your self-worth – a key foundation for a strong serotonin system.

Chapter 8

Clearing Inner Obstacles

Even after breaking up with my toxic ex-boyfriend, he still tried to influence me with his nasty comments. After some time, I had a realisation: his comments were continuing to hurt me, a part of me, deep down, as *I still believed them to be true*. Other people and their words are like mirrors to our wounds.

When there is a belief that you are not enough or that it is not safe to take centre stage and become the main character of your life, anything that another person says that supports these beliefs hurts. For example, comments such as 'you are a terrible mother' or 'you don't have what it takes to succeed in business' feel awful because somewhere, deep within, there is a part of you that believes these things.

Subconscious limiting beliefs are deeply ingrained thought patterns – assumptions that we hold about ourselves, other people and the world around us. These subconscious beliefs are called 'limiting' beliefs, because they can chip away at our self-worth, constrain our potential and limit our ability to achieve our goals and live a life that we dream of. For example, the limiting belief 'I'm not good enough' could impact your personal boundaries in the following ways:

- You may have a hard time asking for a pay rise or promotion at work, even if you know you deserve it.
- You may tolerate disrespectful or abusive behaviour from a partner because you believe you 'don't deserve' better treatment.
- You may avoid setting boundaries around how much you'll do for others because you feel like you have to constantly prove your value and worth.

When you believe you're 'not enough', it's difficult to have the self-confidence and self-respect necessary to set healthy boundaries. You may end up overcommitting, people-pleasing and allowing others to take advantage – all to try to compensate for your perceived inadequacy.

Limiting beliefs are typically formed during childhood or through significant life experiences, and you may not consciously recognise or acknowledge that they even exist. When you have subconscious limiting beliefs they can manifest as self-doubt, fear of failure, feelings of unworthiness or a sense of feeling defeated and powerless. Going back to the common limiting belief of 'I'm not good enough' you might find yourself constantly seeking validation or approval from others. When you don't get the praise you need, you can feel inadequate. As a result, you may feel an urge to do even more so that you can get the praise and reassurance you ache for from friends, family and colleagues. You may fall into perfectionism, setting unrealistically high standards for yourself. The praise that validates your worth – and doing things anything less than perfectly – confirms your belief that you are not enough as you are.

Another deep-seated limiting belief, especially for women, can be a sense of duty, a belief that you need to please everyone around you. As a result, you may seek constant approval from others. This feeling of continuously having to self-sacrifice and neglect your own needs and desires can result in relying on constantly doing things for others for your sense of safety. In the long run, pleasing others as a source for serotonin is not sustainable. When you sacrifice your own needs, you soon won't have the energy you need to blossom. Your needs are there for a reason: so that you can live a life where you not only survive, but have the energy to thrive.

Limiting beliefs can significantly impact various aspects of life, including relationships, career, health and overall well-being. They affect how we see the world, what types of choices we make or whether we pursue an opportunity. Limiting beliefs create internal barriers, while personal boundaries help us set external barriers to protect our authentic selves. Working on both – challenging the limiting beliefs and enforcing healthy boundaries – can be a powerful way to unlock our true potential.

If you want to overcome subconscious limiting beliefs, you need to learn how to identify them, challenge them and consciously adopt more empowering beliefs and attitudes about yourself – and the world around you. Thankfully, your body and mind can help you with this!

Every time a limiting belief is triggered, it causes a stress reaction in the body. Limiting beliefs, such as 'I don't have what it takes,' 'I'll never have money,' 'I'm not worthy,' 'I'm not safe' or 'nothing ever works out' have a way of keeping us small, self-sabotaging and not following through.

There might be patterns that you just can't seem to break that can show the way to a limiting belief that needs healing. You always run out of money. Or maybe you've noticed that you seem to attract people who take advantage of you. For some of you, a sense of loneliness may carry you from one relationship to another. You just don't seem to get where you want to be.

Intense emotions are also a sign that a subconscious belief has been triggered. You may carry a lot of shame in your body, have a sense of powerlessness or find yourself feeling guilty for saying 'no' or setting boundaries. Maybe there is a continuous fear of being rejected, casting a shadow over your life. That fear can express itself in constriction or become part of the feeling of emotional overwhelm that leads to excitation and even inflammation.

When your body talks to you via emotions, sensations, thoughts and memories, I always tell people to listen – it's your nervous system telling you through physical and emotional signals that you are not aligned with your deepest self. Continuous subconscious stress can be a sign that you need to find the route back to yourself.

You can use Emotional Freedom Technique (EFT), commonly known as tapping, to work with your subconscious mind and let go of any limiting beliefs that are preventing you from living your life to the fullest. Tapping is a holistic healing method that combines ancient Chinese acupressure with modern psychology. Tapping has been found in studies to lower stress hormone levels and calm our brain's fear centre, the amygdala. Tapping doesn't replace medical treatment. However, as a coach, through tapping I've witnessed people release negative thoughts, fears and limiting beliefs that had kept them in a downward spiral for years. After I started tapping myself I noticed that, with time, my ex's hurtful words had lost their power. I had healed a limiting belief.

Through tapping, we can calm the activation of our sympathetic nervous system and reprogramme our amygdala's reactions to different situations. The amygdala categorises various objects, situations and sensations as safe or dangerous. With tapping, we can teach our brains not to fear a certain thing anymore. With these new changes in your brain, you no longer feel afraid to go after your dreams and say what you want out loud. You sense in your body that everything will be fine and that the Universe truly has your back.

You can also use tapping to release old pain that is still holding you in the past. It could be a hurtful memory, such as feeling unsupported and unloved or being criticised by a loved one. When an old abandonment or betrayal keeps you from trusting people in the now, you can use tapping to release the surge of energy from the sympathetic nervous system activation. Even frightful memories of a toxic ex bullying, shouting or gaslighting you can be released with tapping.

How to use tapping to clear limiting beliefs

First, identify the specific emotional or physical issue you wish to address. This could be stress, anxiety, a specific fear or any other negative emotion. Find a quiet and comfortable space where you can focus without distraction.

Next, formulate a setup statement that combines acknowledging the issue with self-acceptance, such as: 'Even though I feel [state the issue], I deeply and completely accept myself.' While continuously repeating the setup statement, use your fingertips to gently tap five to seven times on each specific acupressure point, including the top of the head, eyebrows, side of the eye, under the eye, under the nose, chin, collarbone and under the arm. You can tap for longer if you feel like it. Trust your intuition and what feels right at that moment. See the instructional video on my website www.docemilia. com for learning more about this technique and how to do it.

As you tap, express your feelings and thoughts related to the issue. You might feel like crying after the energy of the intense emotion starts to ease out. Crying is our body's natural way of calming itself and lowering stress. Tears even contain stress hormones and toxins, so when you cry, you are quite literally letting go of fear.

After a few rounds of tapping, reassess how you feel and continue the process until you gain a sense of relief or the intensity of the issue diminishes.

Many limiting beliefs stem from feelings of unworthiness, inadequacy or fear. These psychological states are often accompanied by low serotonin levels, which can be seen as a negative, self-critical inner voice. When serotonin is depleted, we also become more susceptible to obsessive rumination, catastrophising and a general lack of confidence in our abilities.

However, by actively working to address and reframe our limiting beliefs, we can take proactive steps to restore balance to our serotonin system and support our overall mental and emotional well-being. As we let go of limiting beliefs and embrace more empowering perspectives, we catalyse a positive feedback loop, cultivating a greater sense of self-worth, resilience and optimism – all of which reinforce the beliefs that serve us best and lead to a healthier and stronger serotonin system.

After we have looked our own fears straight in the eye, befriended them and, with a tool such as tapping, cleared them, we release energy. When our energy is no longer used to fuel intense survival emotions, such as rage, anger, frustration, panic and fear, we can use the energy to go in our own direction and build a new future.

When we clear our fears, we create a larger capacity for joy, relaxation, curiosity, calmness, trust and love.

Over to you

- What fears or worries come up when you think about making a significant change in your life?
- Are there any areas in your life where you feel stuck or like you're not progressing? What beliefs might be contributing to that?
- When you think about your dreams and aspirations, are there internal voices telling you that you can't or shouldn't pursue them?
- What beliefs do you hold that could be keeping you back from achieving your goals or living your best life?
- What messages did you receive growing up (from family, society and so on) that may have shaped your current limiting beliefs?
- Are there any areas of your life where you find yourself making excuses or playing small? What beliefs might be behind that?
- Can you use tapping or other body-based approaches to work with these thoughts and beliefs?

yoga nidra

Creating new neural pathways and letting go of old ones takes energy. You can use yoga nidra to recharge and balance your nervous system if you feel that you want to boost your energy levels and recharge.

I found yoga nidra when there was a lot of stress in my life and the nightly wakeups with a newborn baby made it challenging to sleep and recover during the night. Yoga nidra could help you to boost your energy, create more safety and balance and support your serotonin system.

Yoga nidra is deeply restful *waking sleep*. Studies have shown that a 30-minute practice can be equivalent to two hours of sleep. The yoga nidra practice takes you into a meditative state where your body can recharge its energy levels. The practice can also help with falling asleep more easily, reducing stress levels, creating new neural pathways in the brain and feeling calmer. Even the US Armed Forces use yoga nidra to support recovery and healing. You can go to www.docemilia.com to find a calming yoga nidra practice.

You are enough and worth it

Self-worth is knowing in your body that you are enough. You believe with your every cell that you are worthy of getting what you want and need. You have a warm feeling in your body that tells you that you deserve all the good things in your life – and you don't feel guilty about getting those things.

Once you have learned to let go of the limiting beliefs that are holding you back, you can build up your self-worth to help you live your life unbounded and free. When self-worth is strengthening your serotonin system, you no longer need to find safety in performing a role. It's interesting how quickly our lives can become a performance – trying to be the perfect parent, the successful business person or the dream spouse – and with one foot anxiously in the future and the other ruminating mistakes in the past, you miss actually living your life and being in the present moment.

When you start strengthening your sense of self-worth, you have the energy to express your needs without guilt. For many people, especially women, taking time for only themselves can be hard. With the energy from a more balanced serotonin system, allowing time for yourself can become easier and you may find that you no longer feel it's necessary to justify your needs – not to your partner, your kids or your family and friends. Listening to your needs in this moment is an act of respect and love to yourself that you know will nurture your soul. It becomes a requirement, instead of something that can be negotiated over.

When born into this world, we don't have the capacity to hide our needs: we cry when we are hungry and reach out when we need comforting. To ensure our survival, we rely on others. We need to be loved and to belong as we are, without conditions.

At some point, we learn what makes people accept us. We understand the ways we will receive the admiring gazes we yearn for. We see the expectations the world has on us. And because we need to belong, we start to shape our behaviours so this deeply biological need can be met. You may fear that expressing your needs will lead to rejection or disapproval from others. Maybe you feel that people will judge you or use you to their own advantage if you were to openly express what you want. Maybe you've had past experiences, where your needs have been ignored or dismissed and you've learned to suppress them. Or maybe you have a belief that you should be able to handle everything by yourself because that is what 'strong' people do. People around us start to shape our journeys from early on. And often, we start doing things we feel we should do instead of doing what our hearts tell us to do. But when we hide our needs, we dim our authentic light.

The only person you should try to make proud is yourself.

Our culture is also a strong shaper of self-worth. Cultural norms and values form the standards against which we evaluate ourselves. For example, cultures that prioritise individual achievement may instil a sense of worth based on personal success and accomplishments, whereas cultures that emphasise communal values might place greater importance on contributions to the collective group. Cultural attitudes towards traits such as beauty, intelligence and social status can impact how people perceive their own worth. For instance, in cultures that prioritise physical attractiveness and social status, individuals may equate their self-worth with their appearance.

Social media has a significant impact on both society and culture. On one hand, it has created new ways for people to connect and communicate with each other, regardless of time and physical location. We share ideas and information globally through different platforms. At its best, social media can help us to form important friendships and to feel connected – it becomes a tool for wellbeing.

On the other hand, social media can make us feel more isolated. One study showed that teens who reduced their social media use by just 50 per cent over the course of a few weeks saw major improvements in how they felt about their weight and overall appearance compared with their peers who maintained a consistent level of social media usage. With all the content across feeds, timelines and different social media apps, young people are flooded with images that invite comparison and envy. This can affect their confidence and self-esteem, creating anxiety and making them feel that they are not enough.

And the same thing is true for adults. When you take on the message that you are not enough, you may feel like an imposter, constantly fearing that soon someone might reveal you to be a fraud and that you don't deserve all the good that you have worked for. A weak sense of self-worth can make you feel that you are not worthy of all the success you've gained.

Some symptoms of low self-worth

- You are highly self-critical and focus more on your flaws and weaknesses than your strengths.
- You take feedback or criticism personally and have difficulty accepting it as constructive.
- You shy away from new challenges or opportunities out of fear of failure or not being good enough.
- You constantly seek approval and validation from others to feel worthy.
- You frequently compare yourself to others and feel inadequate or inferior.
- You engage in negative self-talk, putting yourself down or doubting your abilities.
- You often feel like a fraud and are convinced you don't deserve your achievements or successes.

- You may neglect your own physical, emotional and mental well-being, as you don't feel you deserve to prioritise your own needs.

The more you move in ways that you are expected to and the less you listen to your gut, the more stagnant the energy inside you often becomes and your serotonin system remains weak. You were built to dance to the beat of your own drum, and when you follow your heart, you become more aligned with your deepest self.

Over to you

- What are your core beliefs about your worthiness?
- Are your beliefs based on evidence or are they clouded by self-criticism and past pain?
- How can you put in place some small actions from today that will enable you to strengthen and soften your relationship with yourself, to find your deepest feelings and uncover your hidden wounds? How about beginning with five minutes of free-writing now – write down anything and everything that comes into your mind in response to the question: *What am I holding onto within?*

Cultivating self-worth begins with self-compassion and accepting yourself. Take your journal, sit down, look at yourself with honest and loving eyes, and ask yourself the following questions:

- What do I value about myself? What internal attributes (such as kindness or resilience) am I proud of? What external accomplishments are a source of pride to me?
- How do I practise self-care and self-compassion? How do I show myself kindness and understanding during difficult times? How do I take care of my own energy?
- Do I express myself authentically, aligned with my own values and passions (see page 69)? Am I speaking in my true voice?

Talk to yourself with the same kindness you would show a dear friend. Acknowledge your mistakes and failures with acceptance rather than harsh self-criticism and remind yourself that imperfection is a natural part of the human experience.

Below are some additional tips on how to strengthen your self-worth:

- Closely monitor your self-talk and actively challenge any negative, self-defeating thoughts. Reframe those thoughts in a more balanced, realistic way. Replace 'I can't' with 'I'll try my best' or 'I may struggle, but I am learning'. Focus on progress rather than perfection – celebrate your growth and improvements, even if you haven't reached your end goal yet.
- Surround yourself with supportive people who appreciate you for who you are. Limit time with those who are consistently critical or make you feel inadequate. Seek out mentors or role models who can provide encouragement and inspiration.

- Prioritise your physical, emotional and mental well-being through self-care. Engage in activities that help you recharge, such as exercise, meditation or simply taking breaks. Treat your body with kindness and respect through healthy habits.
- Emotional Freedom Techniques (EFT, see page 157) can be used for building self-worth.

Becoming Worth It

Many people have told me that after leaving toxic relationships or workplaces, their heart started to grow again. After breaking free of old patterns and beliefs, you can start your journey of self-discovery. *Am I a morning person or an evening person? What do I really enjoy doing? What do I need to flourish?* Even your body can reflect these changes as you find the route back to yourself again.

For many of us, finding our way back to our own needs and desires can bring a whirlwind of energy. You no longer skip on your workouts because you know that is what you need to be the best version of yourself. You no longer settle for breadcrumbs in your relationships. You protect your energy.

In my case, I needed to learn how to shield my energy when there were people around me who wanted to push me down or hurt me. I needed to recognise and own the fact that I, too, had enjoyed the flux of stress hormones that comes from drama. Even though it felt hard, deep down I knew that this pattern no longer served me and, in the long run, would drain my energy and make me sick. If I wanted to be a good mother and use my energy positively, I needed to get back to myself.

With every step closer to finding your deeper self, expressing your authenticity and sharing your needs, you build up the serotonin system. It strengthens every time you have the courage to face your fears and release old patterns that no longer serve you. With every boundary you put in place and each act of self-compassion, you lower your stress levels and help the nervous system to feel safe.

However, it's important to remember that healing takes a lot of energy. Even when your body finally feels safe, you will feel exhausted. Your body has been in survival mode for so long that it needs time to rest and refill its energy reservoirs. This is nothing to be afraid of. Tiredness is your body's way of signalling that it feels safe enough to just be and recharge itself. After exiting my toxic relationship, I was exhausted for months and I really tried to give my body and mind some well-needed rest – I took long walks in the forest and meditated a lot. I also used yoga nidra to give me an extra recovery boost (see page 160).

Even though some of our biggest pains are inflicted *by* other people, we also do our healing *through* other people. We are mirrors to each other. When the pain is deep, we might need guidance and help from professionals to hold the space we need to confront our fears. We can better go through the pain and heal from it when we are together on our journey with people who make us feel safe.

With every pain you feel and wound you heal, the stronger your serotonin shield becomes. And the stronger your serotonin shield, the less your energy leaks outside – and the less fear, shame, worry or disgust have routes to enter your system. This creates more space for joy, ease, peace and trust. And the more balanced your serotonin system is, the more courage you have to share your superpowers and shine your light to the world.

Dopamine has given you the wings to fly and serotonin the strength to open them. In the next and final part, we'll look at oxytocin, which will give you the roots to come back down to earth and feel connected to everything. This connection makes us trust and feel at peace.

Your to-do list for a sustainable flow of serotonin

- Learn to pause before reacting.
- Know that you are not a prisoner of your past but the creator of your future.
- Try to put things in perspective. Is this something you would worry about in five years time?
- Focus on the things you can change.
- Work on your limiting beliefs. EFT and other somatic techniques can help you remove some of the beliefs that are blocking your way.
- Listen to the pain and its messages instead of just masking it.
- Start telling yourself the story you actually want to hear.
- Set healthy boundaries. Some people won't like it, but in the end it will be best for everybody.
- Start making yourself proud and tell yourself you are enough.
- Be patient and gentle with yourself – inner healing takes energy.

Part 3

Oxytocin: The Hormone of Connection

Chapter 9

What is Oxytocin?

Oxytocin is the hormone of oneness and connection. When flowing in balance with dopamine and serotonin, oxytocin makes you feel connected – not only with yourself but with the people and larger world around you. You might have already heard how hugging a friend, petting a dog or getting a massage can release oxytocin in your system. But if we look deeper into the wisdom of oxytocin, we can see how it helps us *belong*. Oxytocin is both a hormone and neurotransmitter that plays a significant role in various physiological processes in our bodies, such as sexual arousal and childbirth, and is involved in many important behaviours, such as social bonding and attachment. It is oxytocin that after great sex or an orgasm can wash all your worries away and bring that calm sense of peace, contentment and a deep-seated knowing in your body that all is good.

Oxytocin is produced mainly in the hypothalamus in the brain and is secreted into the bloodstream by the pituitary gland through things such as physical touch, positive inter-actions and emotional intimacy. Oxytocin helps us to form lasting relationships and to bond with others and has been shown to have a calming effect on the body, counteracting the physiological effects of stress and anxiety. It can also help reduce cortisol levels and promote a sense of well-being.

We release oxytocin naturally when we are in physical contact, skin-to-skin – a gentle touch, a hug or a kiss all create a flow of oxytocin in our system. Even a cuddle with a pet can support oxytocin release, as can spending time with loved ones, laughing and having worthwhile conversations. Oxytocin loves strong and meaningful connections – with others and with our selves.

Oxytocin promotes relaxation and trust even in our most vulnerable states. It's oxytocin that helps women (and, to a lesser extent, men) to surrender to the pleasure of orgasm and stimulates uterine contractions during childbirth. Oxytocin encourages us to trust that the people around us want good things for us. Through oxytocin, we create strong bonds and connected communities.

Oxytocin can be viewed as a hormonal super-regulator that coordinates all the other love hormones. By influencing the activities of various hormones and neurotransmitters, oxytocin commands a leading position in the body's hormonal hierarchy, essential for both interpersonal relationships and overall health. This means that, if you want to work with, let's say, your cortisol levels or your sex hormones, you can start by working with your oxytocin levels. I will teach you how in Chapter 13.

Oxytocin: The master hormone regulator

Oxytocin sits atop the hormonal hierarchy, acting as a master regulator of other key hormones. Underneath oxytocin sit the 'survival hormones' – cortisol, insulin and adrenaline – which help the body respond to stress and threats. And under the survival hormones we have our sex hormones – such as oestrogen, progesterone and testosterone – in charge of reproductive health and overall well-being. Recent studies propose that oxytocin can also lead to an increase of dopamine in the brain. Oxytocin interacts with serotonin pathways in the brain, contributing to a sense of safety and connection. The relationship between oxytocin and other hormones is complex and multidirectional.

Oxytocin coordinates the interactions between these different hormone systems, ensuring they work in harmony to maintain overall physiological balance and well-being. If you want to work any of the other hormones you should never ignore oxytocin.

Oxytocin is the molecule of connection and trust. Once we feel connected with ourselves and everything around us, we have trust that helps us to open our palms and relax. We believe that we will be held by others when we have the need, and that we will have the capacity to hold ourselves, too. Instead of trying to force things to happen, we trust we are enough and everything will work out. We feel grounded and content, even blissful, as oxytocin makes us feel that all we need is already in this moment. There is no desire to be anywhere else; it feels good to just be. Our minds are clear and we have a strong sense of who we really are.

Oxytocin is not only crucial for social bonding and trust, but also plays a key role in sexual function and desire. That's why pharmaceutical oxytocin has emerged as a potential therapeutic option for boosting low sex drive.

When administered as a medication, oxytocin can heighten feelings of intimacy and attachment, making sexual activity more emotionally fulfilling. This, in turn, can increase arousal, pleasure and the overall motivation to engage in sex. Importantly, the effects of oxytocin-based treatments appear to work best when coupled with activities that promote social connection, such as physical touch and eye contact.

While oxytocin medications show promise, they often come with side effects and some risks, and there are several natural ways to give your body's own oxytocin production a lift without resorting to medication:

- Practise mindful touch, like hugging, cuddling or massage.
- Spend quality time with loved ones. Instead of watching TV, try to engage in activities that include eye-to-eye contact.
- Get enough sleep. Lack of sleep can increase stress levels and disturb oxytocin levels.
- Sweat together. Working out or going to a sauna together can increase oxytocin levels and deepen the bond and promote a sense of genuine connection.

The Dark Side of Oxytocin

When oxytocin does not flow from sustainable sources, you can feel lonely and cling to everything and everybody around you, hoping to feel connected. You may feel that you need to take care of things all by yourself, and it can be hard to trust that others will help you when needed.

When we don't have a sustainable flow of oxytocin to calm us, we often cling to things. Sometimes it's material things that we hold on to – thinking that maybe a new purse or home would make us happy. Sometimes it's relationships. Regardless of the unsustainable source, we still feel empty, trying to fill the void, constantly thinking 'if only' and 'when'.

On a deeper level, I believe that oxytocin flows when you are connected to your most authentic self, so when we become disconnected from our deepest selves, we can't truly connect with the life around us.

When our oxytocin levels are not balanced, life can feel unfair and heavy. It feels as if we are doomed to survive alone and that no one understands what we are going through. The world's weight is carried on your shoulders and you think no one is there to help you. You feel disconnected, alone, watching life pass by. Buried by the thoughts in your head you find it hard to 'be' and may sense a restlessness rising.

My days as an occupational physician in a large Finnish corporation felt empty. Being a doctor and helping people should have given me a feeling of purpose, but I felt like a shitty doctor. I concentrated on taking on as many patients as possible, and I felt as if patients were merely coming in and going out. I didn't have the time to be fully there for my patients, and this made me feel both frustrated and sad. Here

I was, a doctor, trained to help people, but I couldn't be of service to them in the way I truly wanted. I found myself prescribing too many drugs instead of treating the root cause. Deep inside, I felt ashamed and after work, drained. I went out with my friends, trying to have fun, but even though I was surrounded by people, I still felt separate and restless and returned home feeling lonelier than ever. I was constantly living either in the future or ruminating on the past. I barely remembered how it felt to be in the moment and sensed that my life was just passing me by.

I tried to fill the hollowness with people, *stuff*, travelling. Like sticky tape, I clung to everything around me. Yet, the more I had, the more alone I felt. Life felt unfair and hard, and there was bitterness in the air.

We say that 'the eyes are a window to a person's soul'. I recently found a picture of myself from that time when I felt so disconnected from who I was. The hollowness came through even from a photo and as I looked at myself, it seemed like there was no one looking back at me.

I didn't have a sustainable source of oxytocin from being truly connected, and it showed. I felt separate from my own life and, underneath, there was a lack of trust; a trust that I was being held.

I can, however, recall an experience when oxytocin made me feel deeply connected to everything around me. Sitting in the middle of the night in my two-month-old-daughter's room, breastfeeding her. The heightened oxytocin levels in that moment made me so present and fulfilled with life – the feeling that I have it all, *right here, right now*, with no emptiness, no restlessness. I had a sense of peace and joy in merely being. My soul felt full. But eight years after, I kept wondering, *how could I get back there?*

During the rest of that unbalanced time in my life, I was having sex, hugging my kid, taking warm baths and getting regular massages – these all helped me hang in there, but were just a quick fix until I eventually started doing the deeper inner work we're exploring in this book.

If my story resonates with you, do know that there is a way back to the peace and fulfilment that I found sitting with my newborn daughter when my soul felt truly at home.

To feel connected, you need to create an opening. And for many people who have been immersed in the individualistic 'you have to deal with this by yourself' narrative, this can be hard. After all, telling others that you need help can be seen as a sign of weakness, when, in fact, to create a true connection you must learn how to receive. Vulnerability opens the door, and learning how to receive help and love can be the greatest thing for your oxytocin system.

Born for connection

Humans need to be touched; our skin yearns for connection. As beings, we come to full fruition *only by being held*. Without other people as both our mirrors and co-regulators, as babies we simply wouldn't survive.

Research on Romanian orphan children who were never held gives a harrowing idea of how those children not only never develop properly, but often die. During the Ceaușescu regime in Romania from 1965–1989, thousands of children were raised in overcrowded institutions with limited caregiver interaction. This means that many of these children lived their lives in their beds never being cuddled, held, sung to or played with. When they cried, documents show that these children were left to 'soothe themselves' alone.

As a result, the majority, if not all of these children suffered from at least some kind of developmental delays, such as not knowing how to talk or walk, stunted growth, as well as cognitive impairments, such as low IQ and problem-solving skills. Malnutrition was also evident in many of these children, as well as health issues and emotional scars.

We learn how to regulate ourselves and calm ourselves down in challenging and stressful situations, *by first being comforted and regulated by others*. A young baby doesn't have the capacity to soothe themself when in distress; they need an adult, with a more developed nervous system, to help their nervous system to calm down. In co-regulation, the caregiver serves as a secure base from which the child can explore the world and navigate challenging situations. By responding sensitively and empathetically to the child's cues and needs, the caregiver helps the child regulate their emotions and behaviours, teaching them valuable self-regulation skills in the process.

We adults also co-regulate through mirror neurons. Mirror neurons are specialised neurons in the brain that fire both when an individual performs an action and when they observe someone else performing the same action. This means that we can feel what the other person is feeling by just watching them. We start to resonate with each other. For example, kids notice how their parent feels without any words being spoken (the other day, when I was feeling a bit low, my six-year-old son came and hugged me as he felt how I was feeling) or you might have noticed how, in meetings, the energy is contagious – one person can shift the energy into chaos or, conversely, calm and peace. As a result, a calm nervous system can be an inviting anchor for other nervous systems and help them to return back to a sense of safety and calm.

In this section, we'll be looking at how you can create a sustainable oxytocin flow from the inside out – just as we have done for dopamine and serotonin – focusing on the following three areas to strengthen your connection with yourself and others:

- **Connecting to your deepest self:** Only by being connected to ourselves can we truly connect with other people, our direction and purpose. We'll explore how you can draw this straight line of connection between you and your deepest, most true self in Chapter 10.
- **Practising gratitude:** Gratitude is love in a small package. Gratitude has the power to change your perception and create more space, connection and trust in your life; a tiny shift with a potentially big impact. We'll look at ways of bringing gratitude into your life in Chapter 11.
- **Coming back to oneness:** We are all part of nature and the world around us. It can be easy to think that

we are somehow separate from everything, living on our own. But the truth is, we are all connected on energetic and deep biological and cellular levels.

By the end of Part Three, I hope you'll not only have knowledge of some of the latest discoveries in quantum medicine, breathwork and deep meditation, but also some long-term practices you can introduce into your life so that you can find a tremendous sense of peace and belonging wherever life takes you.

First though, let's look at some tools for boosting oxytocin in daily life, which can be beneficial while you are doing the deeper work.

Immediate Oxytocin Support

While you can't consume oxytocin directly from foods or external sources, there are some simple things you can do to naturally stimulate oxytocin production and release.

Strengthen the bond with your partner

We synchronise with others through the sensory nerves of our skin. This phenomenon is often referred to as 'biological coupling' or 'interpersonal physiological coherence'. Several studies have demonstrated that, when a baby is held in skin-to-skin contact with a parent or caregiver, the two individuals' physiological rhythms can synchronise. This synchronisation can manifest in various ways, including the alignment of heart rates, respiratory rates and even brainwave patterns. Our skin – and touch – can be a powerful messenger of connection and trust.

Oxytocin plays a significant role in enhancing sex life and deepening emotional connections between partners. Oxytocin is released during physical touch, such as hugging, kissing and sexual intimacy, and it fosters feelings of bonding, connection and trust. During sex, oxytocin levels surge, intensifying the sense of closeness and attachment between partners. This hormone not only amplifies physical pleasure and emotional satisfaction but also promotes relaxation and reduces stress, creating a nourishing environment for intimacy. Elevated oxytocin levels are also linked to increased empathy and communication, which can further enrich the sexual and emotional connection between partners.

To boost oxytocin levels you can try the following:

- Oxytocin loves skin-to-skin connection. Simple acts like holding hands, cuddling or giving each other massages will give you a nice boost of oxytocin.
- If you don't have a hugging partner, you can try sleeping with a weighted blanket. Weighted blankets lightly press the body and can stimulate the effect of a hug, promoting oxytocin release.
- Sharing meaningful experiences, such as spending quality time together, engaging in mutual hobbies or simply talking and listening to each other also encourages oxytocin production.
- Practising mindful affection – such as looking into each other's eyes, expressing gratitude and giving sincere compliments – can enhance emotional intimacy and the flow of oxytocin.
- Too often we sit together glued to our smartphone screens. Put your smartphones away at the dinner table when you talk about the day. Meaningful

conversations or sharing a meal together can boost your oxytocin levels.

- Helping others can also be a powerful source of oxytocin, for both the helper and the receiver as oxytocin thrives in strong, trusting environments where people are connected.

Take a warm bath or spend some time in a sauna

Studies have shown that exposure to warm temperatures has been linked to increased oxytocin levels, which can contribute to improved mental wellbeing and relaxation. In my native country, Finland, saunas have been a tradition for centuries. Before the Finns had access to doctors, the sauna was described as the 'poor man's pharmacy'. People were born in the sauna, and the dead were prepared for their last journey there. A sauna is a sacred space where people go to connect with themselves and others.

Traditional Finnish saunas use dry heat, with the temperature rising somewhere between 70°–100°C. This is done by burning wood inside the sauna stove. Sauna rocks lie on top of the sauna stove and as the burning wood heats up the stove, it also warms the rocks. Tossing water on the steaming hot sauna rocks releases a pleasant, warm wave of steam called 'löyly', the spirit of the sauna.

In the traditional Finnish sauna, people sit naked as the warm steam travels to every corner. This experience not only melts the stress of the week from people's bodies, but also softens their borders. The sauna and the hot air force you to stop time-travelling in the past or the future and come back to your body – into the now.

Add some mindfulness to your day

Feel the coffee cup in your hands or the water against your skin in the shower. Engaging in mindfulness practices like this has been shown to increase oxytocin levels, promoting a sense of connection and well-being.

Embrace the micro-moments of connection

In our fast-paced, screen-obsessed world, the small, fleeting moments of human connection are easily overlooked, yet they can be a great source of oxytocin. Something as simple as making eye contact and sharing a smile with the cashier at the grocery shop or stopping to chat with a neighbour you pass on the street can inject a much-needed dose of warmth and presence into an otherwise disconnected day.

Try a digital detox

Regularly disconnecting from electronic devices can help quieten the mind and create more space for connection. Reducing screen time can improve mental health and social connections, which are important for oxytocin production.

We are beings born from connection to connection. And if we want to build a sustainable flow of oxytocin, we need to feel connected not only to other people and the world around us, but also to our deeper selves – which we'll explore in the next chapter.

Chapter 10

Connect to Your Deepest Self

You can only be connected to others by first being connected to yourself. By using the tools in this chapter, you can form a recipe for sustainable oxytocin flow that stems from the connection you have first with yourself – and then expands into how you see the entire world.

When I was still searching for balance and medicating myself with relationships, I was aching for another person's touch to calm down my restless mind. I thought of myself as being someone who was just wired this way – only to relax from another person's touch – when, in fact, it had become something I was relying on. The wisdom of oxytocin is that it asks us to look for connection and belonging *beyond* groups and other people, and get back in touch with our deeper selves. One way of doing this is to recognise that you are not your thoughts.

Your are Not Your Thoughts

Oxytocin is the powerful glue, attaching us to the centre of our being. When the attachment is strong, you can feel like you are occupying your entire body. You are fully present. There is peace and a calm sense of being in the moment.

However, when there is disconnection or the connection is loose, there becomes a void space within you. And to occupy this empty space come thoughts.

When there is only a little oxytocin in our system, we often ruminate on the past or worry about the future, finding it hard to feel happy with what we have – always looking for that missing piece; that one piece that will finally make our life complete. We analyse and create scenarios, living more in our heads than in the world surrounding us. Instead of being in the moment and feeling it on our skin, we are held captive by our minds.

Our addiction to our thoughts and continuously thinking about something is wearing us out. As Eckhart Tolle describes in his book *The Power of Now*, when we feel like we have no choice over our thoughts or we feel we can't stop, thinking becomes addictive. We find pleasure in the justification, blame and worrying in our thoughts. But soon, this pleasure will turn into pain. Your mind goes in loops, and you feel as if you are unable to hop off the train.

Your brain is continuously processing information from inside the body: how much insulin your pancreas has created, whether there is pain or tension in your fascia and ligaments, what is the pH level in your body and so forth. Based on this information, your brain comes up with an explanation of your inner state. *Am I angry? Am I excited? What did I do the last time my body was in this state? What did I see when I was in this situation last time?* And your brain always comes up with these explanations based on your past experiences. Your mind is creating the present based on the past.

Let's take an example. You've been drinking a bit too much coffee and have forgotten to drink enough water. As a result, your body is dehydrated and wired. This is a sign of threat to your nervous system and your cortisol levels increase. Your body is in fight-or-flight.

At the same time, your brain is trying to find a reason from the environment *why* you are prepared to fight or run away. Your mind is focused on locating the source of the threat from the environment and it comes up with explanations of what could be wrong. As a result, your mind is flooded with thoughts that are filled with worry, blame or justification. Maybe you are convinced that your boss is mad at you or that you didn't do a good enough job on your last project. Or perhaps your mind starts replaying a fight with your spouse from the night before, and you spend your drive home from work coming up with arguments and nasty replies. As a result, instead of feeling calm when you park on your driveway, you are still wired up from the train of thought you hopped on while driving the car.

However, most likely, nothing is wrong. Your thoughts were created by the stress of dehydration. But for your body, they were real. So, in a way, your thoughts are only a reflection of how your brain interprets your current bodily state.

The first step is to recognise that you are not your thoughts. Minding your thoughts prevents you from spending all your energy on them even though they are not necessarily true.

Yes, your thoughts can feel loud. They can even feel like hijackers, kidnapping you away from this moment and dropping you into the past or future scenarios in your head. But they are not you. You can open the gate to a sustainable oxytocin flow by learning how to observe your thoughts.

First, tune in and start listening to your own thoughts, observing them as they stream through your mind. After a few minutes you might start noticing how, weirdly enough, you are not your thoughts. Soon, negative thoughts start losing their grip on you. After all, these negative thoughts are not you, but only an old programme, like a CD in a music player, going through the same songs repeatedly out of habit. The first time I realised this, I started crying. Finally, I had a way to let go of thoughts that were straining and causing me pain.

When you listen to a thought and become witness to it, you can sense the spaciousness that begins to take place in your mind and body. It's as if all the intense energy of your thinking has been cluttering up your busy mind and now it can gently dissolve. Maybe you even feel a greater presence emerging when you step away and merely start observing the thought.

This spaciousness is your deeper self.

How to observe your thoughts

Next time you experience a worrying thought or keep re-playing a movie clip from the past over and over in your head, just notice the thought:

- Breathe in and observe your thoughts from the outside.
- Are there any recurring thoughts that, up until now, you hadn't even noticed? Inner critic thoughts? Self-defeating thoughts? Harsh comparison thoughts?
- Write down some of the thoughts that appear that may not be serving you.
- See if you can break the cycle. Next time you hear these habitual thoughts, challenge their truth by stepping back and asking yourself:

    o Is there evidence to support this thought, or am I making assumptions?

THE HEALING POWER OF HORMONES

o If my best friend was in this situation, what
advice would I give them?

o What would be a more realistic, balanced way of
looking at this?

In this moment, you are getting a grasp on the deeper
you – the one behind all the thoughts; the one that is
always at peace, connected and has the answers. This is
your deepest and most true self.

Emotional Freedom Technique (EFT) can also
be great for releasing negative thoughts (see
Chapter 8).

The next time you have a distressing thought or start
worrying about the past or the future, take a step back – and
listen. Your mind may bring you thoughts like: *What if my
friends are upset with me? What if I forgot to say something in
that work meeting yesterday?* or *What if I never find the perfect
partner?* Whatever the thoughts, you can rest in the knowledge that you can always free yourself from this ongoing
cycle by listening to it and acknowledging that you are not
your thoughts.

The secret, though, is to hear the voice in your head
without judgement. Start listening to this voice as often as
possible and let it be. Don't try to fix your negative thoughts,
force yourself to think positively or change what the voice
says. Merely observe.

The more you listen to and separate yourself from your
thoughts, the more you strengthen your prefrontal cortex.
This brain region is responsible for regulating emotions,
setting goals, developing plans and organising steps to achieve

those goals. The prefrontal cortex also helps to suppress impulsive responses, distractions or irrelevant information and allows you to stay focused.

Observing your thoughts and thinking about thinking, as cognitive scientists would say, can help you to solve problems better, make it easier for you to switch between different tasks and perspectives, help you to adapt to new situations and break down large goals into manageable steps – and reconnect with your truest self.

Observing the voice in your head and merely letting it be is a beautiful step to bring more present-moment awareness into your days and find that connection again.

Over to you

- Do you feel connected to your true self?
- Who are you behind your thoughts?

Stop Clinging

When we feel connected and have enough oxytocin in our system, when we feel anchored in our body, we are strongly rooted in the present moment – in the now. Instead of analysing our life in our mind, we are feeling and sensing it though our body.

When our oxytocin levels are low, however, and we don't have a strong connection to our deeper selves, we can easily start grasping at the material things around us. Like clingfilm, we attach to any surface near us to feel connected, whether that is people, relationships or things.

Instead of pausing and finding peace and joy in what we already have, we are restless and try to buy our way to peace, always looking for what will make us feel we have it all. We always need something else. Instead of tuning in, we tune out and want to find peace outside ourselves. When in fact, nothing from outside – whether that is a new handbag or a new apartment – can bring the peace that comes from being connected with your deepest self.

We don't recognise that what we are thirsty for is the connection with ourselves.

How to detach yourself from people and things

If you feel like it's hard for you to detach yourself from the outside, try these tips:

- Let people be who they are, and then decide if you want them in your life.
- When considering buying something, pause and question whether you really need it.
- Trust that rejection is redirection to something better.
- Remember that some people are only meant to help you grow, not be in your life forever.
- Focus on the things you can control.
- Accept that some things must fall apart to come together in a new, better way.
- Remember the more balanced your love hormones are, the more you will start detaching from things that don't serve you. Keep doing the work.

The antidote to clinging and attaching to everything is strengthening your connection to your deeper self. The more you are connected to yourself and your authentic needs, the less you need to cling to others for a sense of clarity. When you find the road back to your deeper self, you know who you are and where you stand. You are fulfilled and present in the moment.

Present-moment awareness and presence is your gateway to having it all.

Anchor Yourself in the Present

The wisdom of oxytocin has shown me, time after time, how the act of distancing myself from the movies of my mind and anchoring myself in the present moment is the perfect antidote to restlessness. Learning how to be present in everything that we do is the gateway to tapping into endless oxytocin and strengthening our connection to ourself and others around us.

Presence is your gateway to more fulfilment, joy and peace, to a sustainable flow of oxytocin and to a feeling that you have it all.

Being present doesn't consume your energy. On the contrary, it creates more of it. Continuous thinking and analysing takes up a lot of energy. The more you are present in the moment, the more you can reduce your cortisol levels. You may not only feel more energised during the day but also sleep better at night.

You don't need rigorous yoga practices or to meditate for years to become more present. Instead, there are some simple practices you can try straight away.

Use your five senses

Every day, whenever you notice yourself wandering into negative thought loops and feeling disconnected, use the five senses grounding technique: Think of five things you can see, four you can feel, three you can hear, two you can smell and one you can taste. This will anchor you in the here and now.

Use your breath

Deep breathing exercises can be a powerful way to be in the present moment and find a way back to connection with your deeper self.

I remember vividly the morning after going to a holotropic breathing workshop. I was walking to the coffee maker to make my first mug of the day. Suddenly, I thought, *why?* I felt like the breathwork had cleansed my brain of its old conditioning. Habits didn't seem to have the grip that they normally had. I realised that I didn't really fancy a coffee, it was purely automatic behaviour driving me to the coffee machine. I felt as if I was free to choose. Some even say that breathing exercises can encourage us to tap into the subconscious mind, helping us to clean any old programming that may keep us stuck in our lives. You can imagine new snow falling on top of your old neural pathways, making it easier to see new opportunities and to connect new pathways. This is the power of deep and transformative breathwork; it can give you a new opportunity to choose – not from old pain, but from future hopes.

Holotropic breathing

Holotropic breathing is a powerful technique that aims to induce altered states of consciousness through rapid, deep breathing. Developed by psychiatrists Stanislav and Christina Grof, the process involves participants breathing quickly and intensely, often accompanied by evocative music and the guidance of trained facilitators.

Participants describe profound emotional release, mystical experiences and enhanced self-awareness. The practice has even shown therapeutic promise in addressing issues like addiction, depression and PTSD. By accessing these non-ordinary states, individuals can process suppressed emotions, integrate past traumas and expand their understanding of themselves and the world. A 2013 study published in the *Journal of Psychoactive Drugs* found that participants who engaged in holotropic breathwork sessions showed significant increases in oxytocin levels compared to a control group. The researchers suggested that the altered states of consciousness induced by holotropic breathing may facilitate the release of oxytocin.

However, holotropic breathing also carries significant risks that cannot be overlooked. The intense, forced breathing can lead to hyperventilation, dizziness and even loss of consciousness if not performed correctly. There are concerns about the potential to re-traumatise individuals with a history of abuse or psychological vulnerabilities. Additionally, the cardiovascular strain poses dangers, especially for those with pre-existing heart or circulatory conditions.

Responsible practice of holotropic breathing requires safety protocols, thorough medical and psychological screening and skilled facilitation, and the participants must be closely monitored throughout the process.

To get started with connecting to your breath, you can use straw breathing to support your oxytocin system. Straw breathing is a breathing technique designed to help calm the mind and body by extending the exhale and encouraging slow, controlled breaths. This practical breathing technique involves breathing out through a straw (or simulating this action by pursing the lips), which creates resistance and helps regulate the breath. This technique can reduce anxiety, promote relaxation and improve focus. On top of that, it can help to calm down your nervous system, helping you to ground yourself when the waves of life are too hard, strengthening the oxytocin system and your sense of trust and calm in the world.

Here's how you can practise straw breathing:

1. **Get a straw:** If you don't have a straw, you can simply purse your lips as if you're breathing out through a straw.
2. **Find a comfortable position:** Sit or lie down with your back straight and shoulders relaxed.

3. **Inhale:** Breathe in deeply through your nose for a count of 3–5 seconds, filling your lungs completely.

4. **Exhale through the straw:** Place the straw in your mouth (or purse your lips) and exhale slowly and steadily through the straw for as long as you can. Focus on making the exhale longer than the inhale.

5. **Repeat:** Continue this pattern for several minutes, inhaling through the nose and exhaling through the straw. Practise this breathing technique for 5–10 minutes or until you feel more relaxed.

After any transformative practice, remember to give yourself time and space for new neural pathways and habits to form. Internal work takes a lot of energy and you need space if you want the changes to stick. Just doing the practice is not enough – you need to change how you go about your everyday life. Nothing changes if nothing changes.

Look with new eyes

Another way to feel more present in the now is to try to find three new things about a person or a place. Dr Ellen Langer, the 'mother of mindfulness', suggests that when we actively notice new things, this puts us in the present. And even more, as we are noticing new things, it's literally enlivening us.

Below are a few ideas for how you can start looking with fresh eyes and becoming more present:

- When you go on a walk, leave your phone at home and be present as you walk. Can you hear new sounds in your environment? How does the ground feel under your feet as you walk? Can you smell the air in your nose?
- Notice three new things about your friend or partner as you speak with them. Look at their face and notice how it moves as they show emotions. Can you find any new aspects on their face that you haven't noticed before? Is there something in their appearance that usually goes unnoticed by you? How do they carry themselves? Can you notice new things in the way they move?
- Try something new, like cooking or playing an unfamiliar sport and share three new things about how it made you feel. Pay attention to any new tastes or smells from your food while you eat it.

Presence is your gateway to inviting more oxytocin into your life. When you learn how to distance yourself from the thoughts in your mind, you create more space for things to emerge. On top of seeing the world in a new way and seeing new opportunities, being present helps you to preserve your energy.

Spending our days in our minds and going through endless to-do lists or answering imaginary emails takes up a lot of mental space. As a result, we feel distant from our lives. We feel separate and alone.

However, when you learn how to be present, you are never alone again. You are always with your true self.

Open your vision

Expanding and opening your visual awareness can have a positive impact on your overall well-being and help you connect to the world around you in several ways:

1. When you consciously broaden your visual focus, it can trigger the relaxation response in the body, helping to counteract the physiological effects of stress. This can lead to lower heart rate, blood pressure and muscle tension.
2. Expanding your visual field encourages a more open, receptive state of mind, which can enhance your ability to concentrate and be present in the moment. This can boost productivity and overall cognitive performance.
3. Widening your visual perspective can shift your mindset from being narrowly focused on problems or negative thoughts to a more expansive, holistic view. This can help reduce rumination and promote a more positive, optimistic outlook.
4. When you consciously open your vision, you become more attuned to physical sensations and the environment around you.
5. Expanding your visual field can expose you to new perspectives, patterns and possibilities, stimulating creative thinking and inspiring innovative solutions to problems.

Below are some tips to open your vision:

- Try to gaze softly with a wide, panoramic focus.
- Scan through your environment with a sense of curiosity and wonder.
- Consciously relax the muscles around your eyes and forehead.
- Alternate between a narrow and broad visual focus.

How to Deepen Your Connection with Meditation

Studies have found that various meditation techniques can lead to measurable increases in oxytocin levels. This has been observed in practices like loving-kindness meditation, compassion meditation and mindfulness meditation. Meditation appears to have a regulatory effect on the oxytocin system. Regular practice has been shown to enhance oxytocin receptor sensitivity and improve the brain's ability to respond to oxytocin signals. This can create greater feelings of social connectedness and empathy.

The oxytocin-mediated effects of meditation have also been linked to improvements in social skills, empathy and emotional regulation, and meditation practitioners often report enhanced feelings of trust, compassion and connection.

I introduced the power of meditation in Chapter 6 as a way of lowering your stress levels. On top of introducing mindfulness into my days, even for five minutes, different meditation practices have proved to be highly beneficial on my own journey towards more connection, so I want to explore another meditation practice here that is easy to do, even if you don't have the time to sit down and meditate.

Deep om meditation

The deep om meditation is extremely simple, but a powerful tool in your energetic toolbox. First, find a quiet and comfortable place where you won't be distracted. Then, close your eyes and take a deep breath to relax your body and mind. Release any tension you may be holding in your muscles, starting from your head and slowly moving down to your toes. Allow your body to feel heavy and grounded.

Then, bring your awareness to your breath. Notice the natural rhythm of your breath as it flows in and out of your body. Take a few moments to observe the sensation of each inhale and exhale. Begin chanting the sound 'aum' or 'omm' slowly. As you chant, feel the vibration of the sound resonating within your body. Can you feel how the soundwaves vibrate on your lips? Can you feel your chest echoing the sounds you create?

You can slowly deepen your chant and immerse yourself in the experience. If you find your mind wandering, just slowly bring your attention back to the sound and sensations in your body. You can choose to chant for a specific time or for however long it feels good for you at that moment – some days you may need a longer chant, other days perhaps a shorter chant will bring a sense of peace and calm.

When you're ready to end your meditation, gradually bring your chanting to a close. Take a few moments to integrate the experience and quietly observe any sensations or insights that may have arisen during the practice. Gently open your eyes and return to the present moment with a sense of peace, clarity and bliss.

I use deep om meditation in the shower every morning, repeating the chant seven times to help me start the day from a state of connectedness. Humming activates the parasympathetic branch of the nervous system, reducing stress and helping us to feel calmer. I have found that often it is merely the intention to connect with not only my deeper self but also other people and the Universe around me, that is enough to give me the energetic push I need for more peace, harmony and connection. In addition, we can't think while we are humming, so humming is an excellent way to create space between our thoughts and strengthen the connection with ourselves!

The science behind humming

- Humming has been shown to stimulate the parasympathetic nervous system. This can help counteract the body's stress response and promote a sense of relaxation.
- Humming increases the production of nitric oxide, a molecule that helps dilate blood vessels and improve blood flow. This can lead to reduced blood pressure and heart rate, both of which are physiological indicators of lower stress levels.
- The rhythmic, repetitive nature of humming can have a meditative effect, helping to calm the mind and reduce rumination or worrying, which are common responses to stress.
- Studies have shown that engaging in humming exercises can decrease the body's production of our main stress hormone, cortisol.

- Humming, especially in a group setting, can increase social bonding and a sense of connection, which reduces feelings of isolation or loneliness.

Over to you

- When did you spend some time just being?
- What is keeping you from not doing breathing practices or meditation? Could you give them a shot?

Incorporating these practices into your daily routine, even for just a few minutes, can help promote greater well-being, resilience and an enhanced sense of connection to your deeper self. Once you have a better connection to your deeper self, it becomes easier to feel genuine gratitude and start connecting with everything around you.

In the next chapter, we'll explore how to use this gratitude to further deepen the oxytocin flow, cultivating more peace, happiness and a profound sense of belonging in your life.

Chapter 11

Reawakening Gratitude

We often wait for something outside to change our lives when, in fact, if we are grateful for what we already have in this moment, that gratitude can change everything. After some turbulent years, using the practices that we've explored in previous chapters, I had gained my freedom back. The universe had responded to my prayers and bought me my dream home (at almost half the market price), where I had moved with my two kids. I was staring at the dazzling sea from my balcony. I was at peace, and gratitude was filling every cell in my body. I felt I had everything. Here it was, my LA dream, manifesting in Finland. I didn't need to go somewhere else to find a life that felt fulfilling. The journey was an inside job.

In this chapter, we will delve more deeply into the transformative power of gratitude and how you, too, can use it to enhance your overall well-being, connection and trust, as well as prepare you for oneness.

Gratitude is Love in a Small Package

Gratitude is our natural state. However, in the world that we live in today, we are too busy with day-to-day life and there is no space for gratitude – the soft carpet under your toes, a car that takes you places or a fridge that holds your food . . . these are all great luxuries that we often don't even think about. However, when you learn how to notice these small things every day and feel grateful for what you have, all three love hormones – dopamine, serotonin and oxytocin – start flowing. When we are stressed, our nervous system focuses on seeing possible threats in the environment. When we shift our focus through gratitude, we can calm our nervous systems and create space for love hormones to flow more freely.

When it comes to oxytocin specifically, studies have found that experiencing gratitude can significantly influence oxytocin levels and the functioning of the oxytocin system in the brain. The experience of gratitude can amplify the positive effects of oxytocin administration on measures of well-being and social connection. The researchers proposed that gratitude may enhance the brain's sensitivity to oxytocin signals, leading to a deeper subjective experience of social belonging and emotional warmth.

Gratitude has been found to enhance mental and physical well-being by reducing symptoms of depression and anxiety, as well as helping to lower blood pressure, supporting the body's immune functions and improving sleep.

In many traditions and religions people have used prayer to create space for gratitude. Blessing your food or expressing gratitude at the end of the day before falling asleep is a way to create more connection with what is. There is a great saying by Mother Teresa that sums up the power of gratitude: 'I used to believe that prayer changes things, but now I know that prayer changes us and we change things.'

Gratitude has the power to shift your perception and create more space, connection and trust in your life. You can start with the everyday things. If paying bills sends your stress hormones through the roof, you can try to shift the narrative by feeling grateful that there is a flow of wealth and that you *can* pay the bills. And the most important part, this act of gratitude alone can make you feel more spacious and at peace in this moment.

Often this mental reframe – a regular gratitude practice which can become your default if you practise it enough – can be enough to switch the scale from anxiety and stress to gratitude and acceptance. You will feel more connected to the whole and that your bill and tax paying, everyday cooking, driving your kids around to hobbies or cleaning the home can make you feel more connected to the people around you and support a sustainable oxytocin flow.

As with everything in life, where attention goes, energy flows. And when you pause, take notice and consciously start to practise finding things to be grateful for, you soon find that the things to be grateful for have increased. Just like a muscle, gratitude is a skill that you can strength train. The stronger your gratitude muscle, the more solid the oxytocin flow in your system. The first step is to include a gratitude practice in your day. Like going to the gym or brushing your teeth, gratitude will become a daily habit that supports your hormonal balance.

How to Start a Gratitude Practice

A gratitude practice doesn't have to be complicated. Each morning or evening, count out on your fingers five things that have made you feel happier, that you are grateful for. It can be as small as being thankful for having your umbrella if it was raining, being grateful for your health and the ability to breathe freely or having the time to enjoy a cup of coffee or a good book.

Alternatively, grab your journal and write down the things you are grateful for first thing in the morning. You can use the following questions to guide you:

- What do I enjoy doing?
- What good things have happened recently?
- What is good about my home/children/job/partner?

You don't even need a journal to invite the power of gratitude into your life. You can start your day with gratitude while you are still under the sheets. Instead of starting to think immediately of all the tasks you *have* to do that day, take a pause and come back to your body:

- Can you feel the warmth in your toes?
- How does your belly feel?
- How does the duvet/sheet feel on your body?

After taking this conscious pause and creating a window for more space, think about what you are grateful for this morning. It doesn't need to be anything fancy. You can start with the things around you:

- Can you feel grateful for the bed you are lying in?
- What about the home you are in?
- Can you feel gratitude for all that is well in your life?
- Can you bring your focus to small sparkles of joy and feel grateful for them?

The more we practise gratitude, the easier it will come. And soon, like any other habit, it becomes a state of being. You start living in gratitude, learn to appreciate what you have and feel more content and at peace.

Embrace imperfection

No one is perfect, despite what their Instagram might suggest. It's important to embrace your flaws and imperfections. Instead of striving for perfection, focus on progress and growth and celebrate your successes along the way.

I've found that, more often than not, we move immediately from one thing to the other and don't really pause to appreciate the journey we have already travelled. We place our focus on the next goal or the things we want to change. When you pause daily and appreciate and give thanks for what you already have, you increase the positive energy flow in your life.

The Ripple Effect of Random Acts of Kindness

When was the last time you told your spouse or colleague what you appreciate in them?

Just as creativity encourages more creativity and joy gives birth to more joy, sharing the good you see in others creates further goodness around you.

Performing small acts of kindness doesn't just brighten someone else's day, it can trigger the release of oxytocin in both the giver and receiver. Interestingly, even bystanders who witness an act of kindness can get a boost in oxytocin, inspiring them to 'pay it forward'.

This is why practising random acts of kindness can create incredible cycles of positivity. A single deed can improve the mood and behaviour of everyone involved, fuelled by the power of oxytocin.

So, the next time you have the chance to do a small, thoughtful act, don't hesitate. That simple gesture could be the start of a ripple effect of kindness, connection and happiness.

Share Your Appreciation

Gratitude creates an energetic bridge between you and the people around you. The more you share your gratitude with friends and family, loved ones and complete strangers, the stronger the bridges connect you to the web of beings.

You can try this immediately with the people around you. Tell them what you appreciate in them. You may notice how there becomes more space around your heart. Maybe you even notice warmth in your chest.

One thing to remember: be specific. When you express gratitude, be specific about what you're thankful for. Instead of a generic 'thanks', speak or write as specifically as you can. It could be sentiments like, 'Thank you for your support; it meant a lot to me.'

The next time you go to work or are at home, concentrate on finding things that you can thank your co-worker, partner or children for. Maybe you could thank them for emptying the dishwasher or making you tea? Do you notice a stronger connection between you and the other people forming the more you share this goodness? Do you notice, after a while of consciously doing this, that the act of gratitude becomes more automatic and feels more natural?

Over to you

- What things are you grateful for at this moment?
- When was the last time you expressed gratitude towards someone?
- Are you good at receiving compliments?
- What kind of gratitude practice could you implement into your daily life?

Learning how to feel grateful for what you already have is often an invitation for the universe to give you more. By focusing on the good, you train your brain to start noticing more of these things from the environment. When you acknowledge the good in your life, you invite more positive emotions and experiences.

Gratitude lifts you up and takes you on an upward spiral of expansive energy and joy. The more you find things to be grateful for, the more the Universe will give them to you. And at the same time, you will feel increasingly connected with the people around you.

Frequently, even a small act of recognition can build bridges between people. When you focus on the good, those good things multiply. With every mindful attention to and appreciation of what you already have, you invite more of it. If you can share this gift with others, the stronger the energetic bridges will be between you and the people around you.

Learning how to receive thanks from others can also be a powerful exercise. For many of us – and in my experience, women in particular – it's not always easy to accept thanks. We don't feel worthy of getting good things or we sense we need to work harder in order to receive more. Whatever the case, learning how to accept thanks, compliments or small acts of kindness can strengthen the flow of oxytocin and your own capacity to receive.

Now you have learned how strengthening your gratitude muscle helps you live in the moment, it's time to expand and deepen your connection with everything around you.

Chapter 12

Cultivating Oneness

Modern life can often leave us feeling disconnected – from ourselves, from others and from the natural world around us. This sense of separation can create a host of challenges, both individually and collectively. However, new insights from science are revealing the profound interconnectedness that lies at the heart of reality.

Consider the example of a healthy cell. When a cell is fully integrated with its surrounding tissues and fulfilling its purpose, it thrives. But when that sense of connection and purpose is lost, the cell can become dysfunctional and cancerous. Similarly, as human beings, we are not isolated individuals, but intrinsically interconnected with all of life.

Quantum physics has demonstrated that everything in the Universe is entangled at the most fundamental level – particles, energy and the very fabric of space-time itself. We are not separate from our environment, but woven into the grand tapestry of existence.

In this chapter, we will explore ways to cultivate a deeper sense of belonging and unity with the world around you. By re-establishing the feeling of oneness, you will unlock the sustainable flow of oxytocin and start living a life filled with trust, peace and the lightness that comes from feeling held by something greater.

An epidemic of loneliness

We are living in an oxytocin-deprived world where loneliness and isolation have become a global epidemic. According to the WHO, on average every third person has felt isolated or lonely, and loneliness tends to be higher in developed countries than in developing countries.

Loneliness has a serious impact on psychological and mental health, and its effect on mortality is comparable to factors such as smoking, obesity and physical inactivity. Loneliness, however, is not just the physical absence of other people, but the inability to share meaningful experiences and connect on a deeper level. If you are not engaged in activities and relationships that matter to you, you cannot share things that matter.

I remember feeling utterly lonely when I had lost the connection to myself. I learned that to beat loneliness, I had to start with the inner work (which you have been doing as you've journeyed through this book) and come back to oneness. Only by having a strong connection with ourself can we create meaningful and deep relationships – and the more courage we have to be the truest version of ourself, the easier it is for like-minded people to find us.

> ## Over to you
>
> - Do you feel isolated or lonely?
> - Do you have a feeling that it's 'you against the world'?
> - Are you paying attention to the nature around you?

Coming Back to Oneness

The journey back to oneness starts with the simple things we have explored in previous chapters: meditation and deep breathing, asking who you are and learning to accept yourself. Your first steps on this path may look different from anyone else's, but by taking these small actions, you will slowly come closer to alignment where oneness is the natural state – the state we are all born into.

Meditation

By stilling the mind and turning your attention inwards, you can transcend the illusion of separation and directly experience your indivisible connection to all of life.

During meditation, as you focus on the steady flow of the breath, you can start letting go of your thoughts, emotions and sensations. In doing so, you may glimpse the boundless awareness that underlies your experience and feel a profound sense of belonging and oneness with the entire web of existence.

When you are looking to deepen your connection with yourself, the people around you and life itself, you can try metta meditation. This is a meditation that you can use to cultivate feelings of love, kindness, joy, gratitude and compassion towards yourself and others. Studies have shown metta meditation to increase these high-frequency emotions and reduce low-energy emotions, such as anger and resentment. Metta meditation can also lower stress levels and strengthen connectedness and a sense of purpose.

If you fancy trying metta meditation, sit in a comfortable position and begin by directing loving-kindness towards yourself. Repeat the phrase: 'May I be filled with loving kindness, may I be filled with joy, may I live with ease, may I be free.' Gradually extend these wishes outward, first to loved ones and friends, neighbours and other people you have around you, even extending the sentiment to difficult people and relationships in your life, eventually sending loving-kindness to all beings, animals and plants around you.

With each repetition, visualise yourself and others surrounded by warmth and love. You may notice how a feeling of genuine compassion starts filling you from within. Throughout the practice, maintain awareness of your thoughts and emotions. If you find your mind wandering, gently guide your attention back to loving-kindness.

As you finish the metta meditation, take time to reflect on the experience. Be aware of the sensations you feel in your body and carry these feelings of love and compassion into your daily life. You may soon notice how this seemingly small practice can create a greater sense of connectedness, not only to your deeper self, but also to other beings and the Universe as a whole.

Breathwork

Breathwork practices, such as conscious circular or holotropic breathing (see page 195), can also be transformative. By consciously altering your breathing patterns, you can shift your physiology and consciousness in ways that dissolve the barriers between yourself and others. Many report experiences of melting into the larger field of awareness, feeling a palpable merging with the natural world.

Beyond meditation and breathwork, there are embodied practices that can help cultivate a felt sense of connection and wholeness. Activities like yoga, tai chi and qigong can attune you to the subtle energetic flows within your body and the natural world, allowing you to directly experience your integration with the larger field of energy and intelligence that sustains all of life.

Spending time in nature, engaging in practices like forest bathing, or simply sitting in silence and being present with the more-than-human world can also evoke a profound sense of belonging. When you allow yourself to be fully receptive and open to the teachings of the natural world, you can directly feel that you are a part of creation.

Another simple way to surrender to the natural rhythms of life and come back to oneness is to learn to accept.

Time in nature

Sometimes, we need to create space and change scenery to connect with ourselves. I remember sitting against a massive tree in Portugal, gazing at the stunning valley and mountains rising in the north. Tears streamed down my face as I felt the tree whisper, 'You are held. You don't have to carry all that weight alone. We've got you.' In that moment, nature cradled me, offering profound support.

Each day of my week-long retreat began with an hour of meditation, followed by a slow, mindful breakfast and three hours of silence. Without my phone, I journaled daily and immersed myself in breathwork, dance and art therapy.

The morning after sitting under that great tree, I woke up in my tent and felt my spine open. The pressure that had burdened my lower back since I was 16 suddenly lifted, replaced by a sense of lightness and joy. Reflecting on my life, I realised that my back pain had started when I moved out to live on my own at 16 years old – a manifestation of feeling a lack of support when trying to navigate life. I hugged that younger version of myself who had fought to survive, unaware she was never truly alone, always supported by everything around her.

As this realisation flowed through me, it helped the locks in my spine crack open. Finally, after years of holding on, I relaxed into the trust that I didn't need to carry everything alone. In reconnecting with myself and feeling the oneness with nature, I felt safety return to my body.

Learn to accept

Learning how to accept what is, is a powerful way to invite a sustainable flow of oxytocin and a deeper sense of belonging into your life. If you've ever tried to swim against big ocean waves, you'll know how much energy it takes as you try to fight the water. Soon, you are exhausted and most likely haven't moved at all.

However, when you surrender to the waves and float, you soon notice that the waves will take you to the shore. You harness the energy of the waves and move *with* this energy, not against it. In the same way, acceptance releases any friction and strain from your system and allows energy to flow through you.

I used to spend enormous amounts of energy longing for a love that I thought was lost. I missed ex-boyfriend and wondered whether we had made the right decision to end the relationship. Like a seesaw I was constantly swinging from 'what ifs' and hope to guilt and sadness. Then suddenly, I had the notion: it was okay to miss him. It was okay to love him, even though we were no longer together. I could accept that I had this love for him and carry it with me, without trying to force it to be anything else.

To my surprise, this acceptance set me free. It was as if, in an instant, my continuous loop of ruminating and wondering if I'd made the mistake of my life was replaced by a sense of freedom. Yes, I did still love him. But this change was a gateway to something new. It wasn't an ending, it was a new beginning. There is unlimited potential in every moment, especially in the endings.

Accepting is not throwing your arms into the air and becoming passive in life. Far from it! Learning how to accept doesn't mean you need to become a monk or not pursue or want anything in life anymore. Accepting is merely not fighting against the darkness when it falls and trusting that the sun will rise again.

When we accept the situation as it is, we save energy from fighting a fight we can never win. Allowing that your loved one may not be the person you thought they were releases energy and gives you the opportunity to get to know this person for who they are – and not the one you imagined in your head. Sometimes we build stories of who other people are and see them through rose-tinted spectacles. However, this prevents us from seeing the people around us for who they really are and from building a genuine connection with them.

What I've learned over the decades with love hormones is that acceptance creates more space for energy and alignment. Just as joy promotes more joy, surrendering to what is eliminates unnecessary friction in your energetic system and creates more ease. You start to bloom.

When the energy in you flows freely, you become radiant. Your cells work in an optimal way and you start to glow. Moreover, your innate light starts to glow more brightly, because you are not only aligned and connected with your deeper self, but you are doing what you were meant to do and going in the direction of your soul.

Acceptance brings more space and calm. It's an invitation for more joy, aliveness and feelings of oneness.

Tips for grounding and connecting with nature

- Walk barefoot on earth, grass or sand.
- Hug a tree for a minimum of 30 seconds.
- Do a mountain pose: stand with your legs hip-width apart and your palms raised overhead, facing each other.
- Imagine roots growing from the bottom of your feet, extending into the earth.
- Start paying attention to the moon and the sun.

The emerging field of psychedelics

The emerging science behind psychedelic-assisted practices is quite remarkable. Although at this point, I must point out that working with psychedelics should only ever be undertaken in legal and supervised circumstances. Studies have shown that these substances can catalyse neuroplasticity, enhancing the brain's ability to form new connections and break free from rigid patterns of thinking and behaving. Neuroimaging research has also revealed that psychedelics can reduce activity in the default mode network (DMN) of the brain, the region associated with the ego and our sense of individual identity, allowing for more expansive and holistic modes of consciousness to emerge.

The exploration of psychedelics offers a fascinating and often transformative path for better health and connection. A membrane-like structure separates our conscious experience from the depths of the unconscious. Psychedelics, with their unique pharmacological actions, seem to have the power to displace this membrane, allowing more of our inner world to emerge and become visible. These substances can open a direct channel to the unconscious mind – that mysterious realm within us that so often remains hidden from our day-to-day awareness.

Each psychedelic substance interacts with our neurochemistry in a distinct way, offering a unique journey of self-discovery. But, at their core, they share a common effect – the capacity to connect us with aspects of ourselves that have long been suppressed or ignored. Suddenly, we find ourselves face-to-face with repressed emotions, buried traumas and the wellsprings of our deepest desires and fears.

Studies have shown that the administration of psychedelics like psilocybin and MDMA can significantly increase oxytocin levels in the brain and bloodstream. This hormonal shift may underlie the enhanced feelings of empathy, openness and connection that are commonly reported during psychedelic experiences. MDMA and psilocybin also show tremendous promise in clinical research for their ability to profoundly disrupt normal patterns of perception and cognition and increase feelings of oneness.

Psychedelics have the power to increase oxytocin levels and catalyse a profound sense of unity and interconnectedness, allowing us to see ourselves as part of something far greater than our personal ego-self. Under the influence of psychedelics, we may experience a deep sense of oneness with the natural world, with the cosmos and with the collective consciousness that binds all of humanity together across time and space.

This expansive perspective can be both humbling and empowering. It reminds us that we are not isolated, autonomous beings, but connected to everything. This realisation can help to dissolve feelings of separation, loneliness and insignificance, replacing them with a profound sense of belonging and purpose.

It's crucial to note that the use of psychedelics needs to be approached with the utmost care and respect, with the guidance of licensed and experienced practitioners. Preparation and integration of the experience afterwards with skilled professionals is essential to ensuring a safe, meaningful and ultimately healing journey. Thoughtful intention-setting, the guidance of experienced facilitators and the integration of insights through counselling and reflection can help to maximise the transformative potential of these powerful plant medicines. The use of psychedelics can be profoundly transformative, but also carries risks if not handled with care and intention.

The challenge with many practices is so-called spiritual shopping, where people chase fast fixes and peak experiences to support their healing journeys. Many practices can open a door and help you move faster on your journey, but you still need to do the heavy lifting of integrating the changes into your daily life.

Listen carefully to what feels inviting and let it sink in properly (this can take years) before moving on to the next practice or thing.

You can undertake the craziest mind-blowing trauma release exercise or go on a psychedelic journey, but unless you do the integration work well, nothing is likely to change for the better. The goal is to have all the tools for health and happiness inside you.

Quantum entanglement

As modern science is focusing more and more on the things that we can't see or touch, this Western science and more ancient wisdom are slowly moving closer together. They may speak different languages, but they are helping us to understand how we all work as a system and what creates true balance and well-being. We are, after all, waves of energy.

As the groundbreaking theoretical physicist Albert Einstein put it: everything is energy and reality is only an illusion, albeit a very persistent one. What does this mean? When you look at your hand, it feels solid to you. When you use your hand to stroke the hair of your loved one or take a glass to drink some water, everything seems solid. However, when we go to the atomic level, there is mainly empty space in us. And this seemingly empty space is filled with information.

There is energy pulsating through the Universe, through the galaxies and the stars, through you and me and everything around us. We seem separate, but when we look closely enough, we can't really tell where one starts and the other begins. There is no separation between you and me.

You may have experienced yourself how, out of the blue, your stomach turns, just for you to later find out that exactly at that time a loved one on the other side of the world had been hurt. This may be due to a phenomenon in quantum physics called 'entanglement' which means we can influence each other even if we are separated by distance.

Over to you

- Have you ever felt a strong intuitive connection to the well-being or state of mind of a loved one?
- Do you often have synchronicities in your daily life?

The links between quantum principles, the neuroscience of oneness and the role of oxytocin are fascinating. This is an exciting frontier in the emerging world of quantum medicine.

As we deepen our understanding of these interconnected phenomena, we may unlock incredible new ways to help people access profound experiences of unity, empathy and letting go of the ego.

For example, some approaches might use oxytocin-boosting compounds, tapping into the 'love' hormone's ability to dampen self-centred thinking and foster a greater sense of connection. Other therapies could leverage quantum principles like entanglement, harnessing the holistic, non-local aspects of reality to shift consciousness.

The future of this field is brimming with possibility. I believe these kinds of therapies have immense potential to expand human awareness and reconnect us to the fundamental oneness at the heart of existence.

When life feels heavy and unfair, it's often because we've lost our connection to ourselves and our surroundings. We create a shield to protect us, but it makes us forget the most fundamental truths: that we are connected to everything and that life is on our side. But this disconnection is not permanent. We can all find our way back, rediscovering the abundance and miracles that surround us constantly. It's not a matter of 'if' but 'when'. All it takes is the embrace of the journey, the willingness to discard the shield and rediscover our true nature. Take heart and trust the process. If I can make that journey, so can you. The path back to alignment is not a distant dream; it's always available, waiting for you to take those first small, unique steps.

When you start living an aligned life, you drop the unconscious stress and your hormone system is able to function as it was designed to – in a balanced flow of love hormones.

Your to-do list for a healthy flow of oxytocin

- Start listening to your thoughts.
- Connect with the nature around you. Feel the ground under your feet and look at the trees. Pay attention to the sun and the moon.
- Try replacing 'I *have* to' with 'I *get* to'.
- Learn to receive.
- Try to start a short daily meditation practice. Only five minutes a day can work miracles!
- If you have the resources, participating in a workshop or retreat can provide time and space for deepening your connection.
- Try to find your tribe. And often the more authentic version of yourself you are being, the more readily they will find you and support you on your journey.
- Trust that, as you are reading this, you are on the right path.

Chapter 13

The Healing Power of Love Hormones

When your dopamine (direction), serotonin (safety) and oxytocin (connection) flow in balance, when you are following the direction of your heart and have created enough safety to build healthy boundaries and knock down walls of fear, you will start living in a state of connection and love.

Step by step, you become a supercharger of light and have the courage and energy to go after your dreams and express your uniqueness, inspiring others to do so, too. You are no longer afraid to spread your wings and fly. You know that what makes you different is your superpower and your gift to the world. And, as you express yourself more and more authentically, you know that you are representing the Universe in your own unique way and inspiring others to do so, too.

When your oxytocin levels are in balance with dopamine and serotonin, you feel like you are on the right path. You are fulfilling your purpose and find meaning in all that you do.

When you have strong roots, you can endure the storms without breaking down. The life force inside is strong, you are radiant and ready to finally be at one with nature's own cycle.

Embracing the Cyclical Nature of Life

We all have a natural daily energetic cycle. When we wake up, the stress hormone cortisol kicks the day off. After a good night's sleep and starting your day with the morning sun rather than looking at a screen, your energy levels get an energetic boost from their environment, enabling them to rise. Your body is ready to take on the day's adventures, curious about what will unfold and what you might experience.

In the afternoon, there is often a moment of lower energy due to various factors, such as your natural circadian rhythm, declining cortisol and your blood sugar levels after lunch. Instead of accepting and surrendering to this natural state, many of us are driven by our modern culture of productivity and try to push through our slump. We may find it challenging to be in this low-energy state and, instead of taking a small break or giving ourselves a breather, many of us treat ourselves harshly and pour that third cup of coffee. We expect to be in a consistent energetic state throughout the day, so we fight what *is* and create even more friction within our system by using our energy to fight the current and swim upstream. By bedtime, we are exhausted and often frustrated because the day didn't go as we expected it to.

Often, we try to force our bodies' cyclical nature to fit our ideals and cultural expectations of how our bodies and minds work. We expect to be extremely productive and alert throughout the day because, in our culture, the myth of an employee always performing at a high level is still idolised – a constant level of achievement that we all try to reach. Why? Because we think this is normal and instead of listening to our bodies and giving them the rest that they need, we see a dip in energy as a sign of weakness, something we should have a grip on and push through.

> Nothing in nature blooms all year long. Don't expect yourself to.

But what if you could learn how to accept yourself just as you are, instead of forcing your body into a state of being that is not innate to it? Just like an inhale is followed by an exhale, periods of expansion and active doing should always be followed by rest and nourishment. This is part of the balance. Even the nervous system gets exhausted by continuous sympathetic activation and hits the brakes to save energy. We can't be continuously 'on'. We also need to rest and recharge our energy reservoirs.

We all have our unique, innate natural energy levels. You can't compare yourself to how active or how much someone else seems to do throughout the day. We all go through life at our own energetic pace; some have seemingly more energy and enjoy spending it on conquering the world, while others feel that a slower pace in life is their true innate rhythm.

When we challenge the current way of looking at the world and the innate wisdom in our bodies, we start to see how a part can be understood only in its relation to the whole. For example, we often think of cortisol as 'bad' because of its reputation as one of the main stress hormones. However, cortisol is in control of the sleep–wake cycle, as well as regulating our metabolic functions and suppressing inflammation in the body.

Stress is not innately evil. Stress hormones tell us that we are moving towards something and we need cortisol and sympathetic activation to pursue our dreams and create meaningful direction in life. However, it's all about the balance and how much time we spend in the sympathetic fight-or-flight mode compared to the recharging rest and digest state.

The body as a system is in a constant state of transformation; in a harmonious flow of supporting and repairing, growing and expanding. When we fight these currents, we may be the ones stepping in our own way. We are letting our ideals and beliefs on how things 'should' work blur our vision, block our ears and prevent us from hearing what our bodies actually need in a given moment.

By understanding and accepting the cyclical nature of life you can start living 'with the current', which decreases stress hormone production and increases all three love hormones.

In the end, it's all about balance: spending enough time in rest-and-digest and doing nothing. (And when I say nothing, I mean *nothing* – lying on the sofa and scrolling on your phone is not giving your body and mind the rest it needs during the day or truly recharging your system!) Even the things you love doing take energy – if you want true balance, remember to give your system enough opportunities to rest and recharge.

Also, look where you *use* your energy. Using your energy on things that are aligned with your deeper self will always nourish your energetic system – and your soul, bringing you closer to the source of your energy.

Connection to the Source of Your Energy

I've come to believe that instead of us having a finite amount of energy and being afraid of using it for the wrong things, when we feel connected to the deepest part of our selves and understand that we are important parts of nature and the system as a whole, we have all the energy we need to do the things we were meant to do. When oxytocin, dopamine and serotonin are flowing in balance, we move in the right direction in life, we no longer do things from a place of fear and we have the courage to follow our hearts. The more we strengthen our connection with the source of our energy and invite more oxytocin and peace into our daily actions, the more we have just the right amount of energy to fulfil our soul's purpose and become superchargers.

Developmental Biologist Michael Levin, PhD, and his team's work beautifully demonstrates how there is a collective intelligence guiding our life – and even what shape our cells take. The process of a single egg becoming a human with all its creativity and brainpower is guided by bioelectricity.

Bioelectric signals are an important part of regulating cell identity during development. This means that a certain energetic frequency can be a push for a cell to become a skin cell and form the outer layer of your body – or a retina cell, being a part of and contributing to forming your eye. It's the energetic frequency that guides the cell to take on an identity, a spirit of its own.

Cells have goals and they work together towards these goals. They take action and solve problems, convincing other cells to work with them. And when a cell loses touch with its true identity, it no longer knows where it belongs. These cells can become cancerous, eating their way through different tissues and organs, penetrating and creating havoc through the body. Just as cells need to be connected to their purpose to be healthy, so do we. We must follow our own energetic frequency so that we can become who we were meant to be – and fulfil our potential.

You can think of the wisdom of dopamine, serotonin and oxytocin guiding your way back to your own innate frequency. It's as if your entire being pulsates to its own divine rhythm.

Maybe you can recall a moment in your life when someone stepped into the room and changed the entire energy in a matter of seconds. No words, nothing that seemed special – just someone entering a space. Yet, their energy made you feel at ease and their comfort in their own skin inspired you to expand while you were in their presence.

When you stay true to your own frequency, you are fulfilling a bigger purpose in the web of creation. When you stay true to yourself and dance to the rhythm of your own heart, the people who need to find you can find you. When you try to be something you are not, you are fighting against yourself.

Aligned with your deepest self and connected to the source, your being changes. You are at ease, feeling connected to everything and everybody around you. Your love hormones are balanced and you vibrate on your own unique frequency and shine your light. This is the healing power of love hormones.

Final Word

When your love hormones are in balance, you create more magic in your life. You have found your soul's direction, and dopamine flows steadily as you walk on a path of meaning. You feel alive yet content and grounded, surrounded by peace and trust. Your heart is soft and open because you have created boundaries to protect your energy and knocked down the walls that have kept you from connecting with others. You have a mysterious inner knowing that you are in the right place, doing what you are meant to do. And on top of that, others can help you on your path. Because when you dare to show up as who you *truly* are, the people looking for you can find *you*.

When I learned to listen to the questions dopamine, serotonin and oxytocin were asking me, I realised I didn't need to fit into a box – there are no boxes! When your love hormones are in balance, instead of fear driving you, your soul guides you, bringing more energy.

Ten years ago, when I first dove into the research on dopamine, serotonin and oxytocin, my hypothesis was that love hormones flowing in balance can prevent addictive behaviours. However, I also used to believe that, once an addict, always an addict. It's only through my own experience that I no longer perceive this to be true. Once we understand the root causes behind our addictive behaviours we can change. Looking back at myself during those times of imbalance in my life is like looking at a different person. So much has changed. The addictive urges and destructive behaviours are gone. My back pain has gone, together with the mental symptoms. I have changed and it brings me so much joy that my work is also used to treat addictions in a clinical setting. The power of love hormones are truly going to change medicine!

I believe that daring to follow your joy will lead you to places you couldn't even have dreamed of. Like magic, things start to happen. You no longer need to push or force things to move forward; eventually, everything just falls into place. Synchronicities start to happen. Small miracles drop on your doorstep.

When we learn to listen to the wisdom of our love hormones, we develop an internal navigation system. This navigation system helps us get back on our own track when we have taken the wrong exit and found ourselves on someone else's path entirely. The love hormones can guide you back to yourself. You start living in love, and this love is an invitation for more magic.

When all three love hormones are flowing in balance from sustainable sources, your brain becomes more malleable than ever. This means that, when you learn how to 'live in love', you have the power to change your brain – and become the person you were created to be!

Learning how to align with your deepest self and live in a balanced flow of dopamine, serotonin and oxytocin doesn't mean there will never be challenges ahead. Even though love hormones helped me to get rid of my symptoms and to create a life where there is more ease, joy and meaning, nothing in life is stagnant. There are times when I get lost from my own path just to find the same symptoms creeping up again.

However, I've learned to listen to the messages when they are only whispers – instead of driving full speed into the wall, like I did before.

Imbalance is part of a balanced life. And it's only through wandering and stepping off your path from time to time that there is an opportunity to find your way back – with a bag full of new experiences, learning and wisdom to share with others.

Educating yourself in how to balance your love hormones is deep inner work, and I believe that we all need self-compassion during this journey. You are learning how to make better decisions for yourself, letting go of old pain, healing yourself and starting to build a life that nourishes you and makes you feel alive. In my eyes, you are a rock star – and I hope you see yourself the same way!

I hope this book has brought you an understanding of your body and your hormones, a deeper compassion for yourself as you have learned more about why you act the way you do. I hope you have the tools to override any negative habitual patterns you have created and discover your new paradigm for thriving. My wish is that it has lit a spark in your soul for the best journey of your life; the journey of finding your way back to your truest, deepest and most magnificent self.

Thank you for being with me through the pages of this book. I am so excited for your future where you feel vibrant, fulfilled and confident about the gifts that you have to offer this world.

Resources

For more information on me and my work and tools for your healing journey, please go to www.docemilia.com or follow me on Instagram: @DocEmilia

Further Reading

Books

Barrett, L. F., *How Emotions Are Made: The Secret Life of the Brain* (Houghton Mifflin Harcourt, 2017)

Chopra, D. and Tanzi, R. E., *Super Genes: Unlock the Astonishing Power of Your DNA for Optimum Health and Well-Being* (Harmony Books, 2015)

Dana, Deb, *Anchored: How to Befriend Your Nervous System Using Polyvagal Theory* (Sounds True, 2021)

Fredrickson, Barbara, *Positivity: Groundbreaking research reveals how to embrace the hidden strength of positive emotions, overcome negativity, and thrive* (Crown Publishers/Random House, 2009)

Gilbert, E., *Big Magic: Creative Living Beyond Fear* (Riverhead Books, 2015)

Hendricks, G., *The Big Leap: Conquer Your Hidden Fear and Take Life to the Next Level* (HarperOne, 2010)

Kaufman, S. B. and Gregoire, C., *Wired to Create: Unraveling the Mysteries of the Creative Mind* (Tarcherperigee, 2015)

Gottfried, S., *The Autoimmune Cure: Healing the Trauma and Other Triggers That Have Turned Your Body Against You* (Harves, 2024)

Graziano Breuning, Loretta, *Habits of a Happy Brain* (Adams Media, 2016)

Land, George and Jarman, Beth, *Breakpoint and Beyond: Mastering the Future Today* (HarperCollins, 1992)

Lembke, A., *Dopamine nation: Finding balance in the age of indulgence* (Dutton Books, 2021)

Levine, P. A., *In an Unspoken Voice: How the Body Releases Trauma and Restores Goodness* (North Atlantic Books, 2010)

Levine, P. A., *Trauma and memory: Brain and Body in a Search for the Living Past: A Practical Guide for Understanding and Working with Traumatic Memory* (North Atlantic Books, 2015)

Lieberman, D. and Long, M., *The Molecule of More: How a Single Chemical in Your Brain Drives Love, Sex, and Creativity – and Will Determine the Fate of the Human Race* (BenBella Books, 2018)

Maté, G., *In the Realm of Hungry Ghosts: Close Encounters with Addiction* (North Atlantic Books, 2010)

Maté, G., *When the Body Says No: Understanding the Stress-Disease Connection* (John Wiley & Sons, 2003)

Ogden, P., Minton, K. and Pain, C., *Trauma and the Body: A Sensorimotor Approach to Psychotherapy* (W. W. Norton & Company, 2006)

Ortner, N., *The Tapping Solution: A Revolutionary System for Stress-free Living* (Hay House, 2013)

Pert, C., *Your Body is Your Subconscious Mind* audiobook (Sounds True Inc., 2004)

Porges, S. W. and Porges, S., *Our Polyvagal World: How Safety and Trauma Shape Us* (W. W. Norton & Company, 2023)

Porges, S. W., *The Polyvagal Theory: Neurophysiological Foundations of Emotions, Attachment, Communication, and Self-regulation* (W. W. Norton & Company, 2011)

Siegel, D. J. *IntraConnected: MWe (Me + We) as the Integration of Self, Identity, and Belonging* (W. W. Norton & Co, 2022)

Swart, T., *The Source: Open Your Mind, Change Your Life* (Vermilion, 2020)

Web links

Tonkin, T., 'Burnout Hits Record High' *British Medical Association (BMA)*, (2022, June 16). Retrieved from www.bma.org.uk/news-and-opinion/

Chasing Consciousness (2023, Oct 31). BIOELECTRICITY & THE BLUE-PRINTS OF LIFE – Michael Levin PHD #49 [Audio podcast episode]. In Chasing Consciousness Podcast.

Land, George, 'The Failure of Success' *TEDx Talks*. (*TEDxTucson* 2017, January 27, 2017). *The Failure of Success | George Land | TEDx-Tucson* [Video]. YouTube. https://www.youtube.com/watch?v=ZfKMq-rYtnc

American Medical Association. (n.d.). 'What is physician burnout?' *American Medical Association (AMA)*, (no date) Retrieved from https://www.ama-assn.org/practice-management/physician-health/what-physician-burnout

References

Dopamine

Allen, John, 'Creativity, the Brain, and Evolution', *Psychology Today* (2010) https://www.psychologytoday.com/gb/blog/lives-the-brain/201004/creativity-the-brain-and-evolution
https://www.reviews.org/mobile/cell-phone-addiction/
https://www.uswitch.com/mobiles/studies/mobile-statistics/

Bäckman, Lars et al., 'Effects of Working-Memory Training on Striatal Dopamine Release', *Science* (5 Aug 2011): 718. https://science.sciencemag.org/content/333/6043/718

Bloomfield MA, McCutcheon RA, Kempton M, Freeman TP, Howes O. 'The effects of psychosocial stress on dopaminergic function and the acute stress response', Elife. 2019 Nov 12;8:e46797. doi: 10.7554/eLife.46797. PMID: 31711569; PMCID: PMC6850765.

Bromberg-Martin ES, Matsumoto M, Hikosaka O. 'Dopamine in motivational control: rewarding, aversive, and alerting', in *Neuron*. 2010 Dec 9;68(5):815-34. doi: 10.1016/j.neuron.2010.11.022. PMID: 21144997; PMCID: PMC3032992.

Bukowski, C., 'Poem to Nobody', *The Last Night of the Earth Poems*, (HarperCollins, 1992)

Carruthers, Peter, 'Human creativity: its cognitive basis, its evolution, and its connections with childhood pretence', *University of Maryland* (2002) http://faculty.philosophy.umd.edu/pcarruthers/Creative-thinking.htm

Chun, Ji-Won et al., 'Role of Frontostriatal Connectivity in Adolescents With Excessive Smartphone Use', *Frontiers of Psychiatry* (2018) https://doi.org/10.3389/fpsyt.2018.00437

Elliot, Andrew J. et al., 'Handbook of Color Psychology', *Cambridge University Press* (2015) https://psycnet.apa.org/record/2016-09857-000

Flaherty, Alice W., 'Frontotemporal and Dopaminergic Control of Idea Generation and Creative Drive' *Journal of Comparative Neurology* (2005) https://www.ncbi.nlm.nih.gov/pmc/articles/PMC2571074/

Gabora, L. and Kaufman, S. B., 'Evolutionary Perspectives on Creativity' in *The Cambridge Handbook of Creativity* (Cambridge University Press, 2010): 279–300 https://arxiv.org/pdf/1106.3386.pdf

Knecht, Stefan et al., 'Levodopa: Faster and Better Word Learning in Normal Humans', *Annals of Neurology* (2004) https://doi.org/10.1002/ana.20125

Mirowsky, John and Ross, Catherine E., 'Creative Work and Health', *Journal of Health and Social Behaviour* (2007) https://journals.sagepub.com/doi/10.1177/002214650704800404

Sharot, Tali et al., 'Dopamine Enhances Expectation of Pleasure in Humans', *Current Biology* (2009) https://www.cell.com/current-biology/fulltext/S0960-9822(09)01844-2

Waldinger, Robert, 'What Makes a Good Life? Lessons from the Longest Study on Happiness', *TED Talk* (2015) [video] https://youtu.be/8KkKuTCFvzl

Waldinger, Robert and Schulz, Marc, 'What's Love Got to Do With It? Social Functioning, Perceived Health, and Daily Happiness in Married Octogenarians', *Psychology and Aging* (2010) https://psycnet.apa.org/doi/10.1037/a0019087

Wise, R. 'Dopamine, learning and motivation', in *Nat Rev Neurosci* 5, 483–494 (2004). https://doi.org/10.1038/nrn1406

Serotonin

Bennie, Jason A. et al., 'Associations between aerobic and muscle-strengthening exercise with depressive symptom severity among 17,839 U.S. adults', *Preventive Medicine* (2019): 121–127 https://doi.org/10.1016/j.ypmed.2019.02.022

Berger, Miles et al., 'The Expanded Biology of Serotonin', *Annual Review of Medicine* (2009): 355–366 https://doi.org/10.1146/annurev.med.60.042307.110802

Chun, Ji-Won et al., 'Role of Frontostriatal Connectivity in Adolescents With Excessive Smartphone Use', *Frontiers of Psychiatry* (2018) https://doi.org/10.3389/fpsyt.2018.00437

Corliss, Julie, 'Mindfulness meditation may ease anxiety, mental stress', Harvard Health Publishing (2014) https://www.health.harvard.edu/blog/mindfulness-meditation-may-ease-anxiety-mental-stress-201401086967

Davidson, Richard J. et al., 'Alterations in Brain and Immune Function Produced by Mindfulness Meditation' *Psychosomatic Medicine* (2003) https://doi.org/10.1097/01.psy.0000077505.67574.e3

Dias, B. G., and Ressler, K. J., 'Parental olfactory experience influences behavior and neural structure in subsequent generations' in *Nature Neuroscience*, 17(1), 89-96, (2014) https://doi.org/10.1038/nn.3594

Drouin, Michelle et al., 'Phantom vibrations among undergraduates. Prevalence and associated psychological characteristics', *Computers in Human Behavior* (2012): 1,490–1,496 https://www.sciencedirect.com/science/article/pii/S0747563212000799

Field, Tiffany et al., 'Cortisol decreases and serotonin and dopamine increase following massage therapy', *International Journal of Neuroscience* (2004): 1397–1413 https://doi.org/10.1080/00207450590956459

Greenfield, David, 'Tips for Electronic Etiquette and Mindful Technology Use', The Center for Internet and Technology Addiction, 2017

Goyal, Madhav et al., 'Meditation Programs for Psychological Stress and Well-being. A Systematic Review and Meta-analysis', *JAMA Internal Medicine* (2014): 357–368 https://jamanetwork.com/journals/jamainternalmedicine/fullarticle/1809754

Inagaki, Tristen et al., 'The Neurobiology of Giving Versus Receiving Support The Role of Stress-Related and Social Reward–Related Neural Activity' *Psychosomatic Medicine* (2016): 443–453 https://doi.org/10.1097/PSY.0000000000000302

Inagaki, Tristen et al., 'Neural Correlates of Giving Social Support: Differences Between Giving Targeted Versus Untargeted Support', *Psychosomatic Medicine* (2018): 724–732 https://doi.org/10.1097/PSY.0000000000000623

Killingsworth, Matthew and Gilbert, Daniel, 'A Wandering Mind is an Unhappy Mind', *Science* (12 November 2010): 932 www.sciencemag.org/cgi/content/full/330/6006/932/DC1, http://www.danielgilbert.com/killingsworth%20&%20gilbert%20(2010).pdf

Kiser, Dominik et al., 'The reciprocal interaction between serotonin and social behaviour', *Neuroscience & Biobehavioral Reviews* (2012) https://doi.org/10.1016/j.neubiorev.2011.12.009

Korb, Alex, 'Marshmallows and Monoamines The neurochemistry of will-power', *Psychology Today* (2011) https://www.psychologytoday.com/us/blog/prefrontal-nudity/201110/marshmallows-and-monoamines

Kurtz, Jaime & Lyubomirsky, Sonja, 'Toward a durable happiness. Kirjassa Praeger perspectives', *Positive psychology: Exploring the best in people*, Vol. 4. Pursuing human flourishing. Praeger Publishers/ Greenwood Publishing Group, 2008

Lawton, Ricky N et al., 'Does volunteering make us happier, or are happier people more likely to volunteer? Addressing the problem of reverse causality when estimating the wellbeing impacts of volunteering', *Journal of Happiness Studies* (2020): 599–624 https://doi.org/10.1007/s10902-020-00242-8

Ma, Xiao et al., 'The Effect of Diaphragmatic Breathing on Attention, Negative Affect and Stress in Healthy Adults', *Frontiers of Psychology* (2017) https://doi.org/10.3389/fpsyg.2017.00874

Moran, Rosalyn et al., 'The Protective Action Encoding of Serotonin Transients in the Human Brain', *Neuropsychopharmacology* (2018) https://www.nature.com/articles/npp2017304

Nummenmaa, Lauri: Tunnekirjasto: Kuinka tunteet tekevat meista ihmisia. Tammi, 2019. ISBN 9789520405946

Qin, Dong-dong et al., 'Prolonged secretion of cortisol as a possible mechanism underlying stress and depressive behaviour', *Nature* (22 June 2016) https://www.nature.com/articles/srep30187

Ramirez, Steve et al., 'Activating positive memory engrams suppresses depression-like behaviour', *Nature* (17 June 2015): 335–339 https://www.nature.com/articles/nature14514

Saxbe, Darby E. and Repetti, Rena, 'No Place Like Home: Home Tours Correlate With Daily Patterns of Mood and Cortisol', *Personality and Social Psychology Bulletin* (2009) http://psp.sagepub.com/content/36/1/71

Schwartz, Carolyn E. and Sendor, Rabbi Meir, 'Helping others helps oneself: response shift effects in peer support', *Social Science & Medicine* (1999): 1563–1575 https://www.sciencedirect.com/science/article/abs/pii/S0277953699000490

Social media use increases depression and loneliness. University of Pennsylvania, 2018 https://penntoday.upenn.edu/news/social-mediause-increases-depression-and-loneliness

Sundman, Ann-Sofie et al., 'Long-term stress levels are synchronized in dogs and their owners', *Scientific Reports* (2019) https://www.nature.com/articles/s41598-019-43851-x

Tabassum, Faiza et al., 'Association of volunteering with mental well-being: a lifecourse analysis of a national population-based longitudinal study in the UK', *BMJ Open* (2016) http://dx.doi.org/10.1136/bmjopen-2016-011327

Tafet, Gustavo E. et al, 'Correlation between cortisol level and serotonin uptake in patients with chronic stress and depression', *Cognitive, Affective, & Behavioral Neuroscience* (2001): 388–393 https://doi.org/10.3758/CABN.1.4.388

Tawakol, Ahmed et al., 'Relation between resting amygdalar activity and cardiovascular events: a longitudinal and cohort study', *The Lancet* (2017) https://doi.org/10.1016/S0140-6736(16)31714-7

Virginia Tech: Keep calm and carry on; 'Scientists make first serotonin measurements in humans' *Medicalxpress* (30 April 2018) https://medicalxpress.com/news/2018-04-calm-scientists-serotonin-humans.html

Oxytocin

Affective touch and its effects on the oxytocin system. Research Project between 2015–2020. University of Skovde/School of Health Sciences https://www.his.se/en/research/digital-health-research-dhear/translational-medicine-trim/affective-touch-and-its-effects-on-theoxytocin-system/

Algoe, Sara B. and Way, Baldwin M., 'Evidence for a role of the oxytocin system, indexed by genetic variation in CD38, in the social bonding effects of expressed gratitude', *Social Cognitive and Affective Neuroscience* (2014): 1855–1861 https://doi.org/10.1093/scan/nst182

Boer, Diana and Abubakar, Amina, 'Music listening in families and peer groups: benefits for young people's social cohesion and emotional well-being across four cultures', *Frontiers in Psychology* (2014) https://www.frontiersin.org/articles/10.3389/fpsyg.2014.00392/full

Bostrom, Adrian et al., 'Hypermethylation-associated downregulation of microRNA-4456 in hypersexual disorder with putative influence on oxytocin signalling: A DNA methylation analysis of miRNA genes', *Epigenetics* (2019) 145–160 https://www.tandfonline.com/doi/10.1080/15592294.2019.1656157

Brooks, Arthur C., 'Choose to Be Grateful. It Will Make You Happier', *The New York Times* (2015) https://www.nytimes.com/2015/11/22/opinion/sunday/choose-to-be-grateful-it-will-make-you-happier.html

Dias, B. G., and Ressler, K. J., 'Holotropic breathwork: A review of the literature', *Journal of Psychoactive Drugs*, 45(4), 307-316 https://doi.org/10.1080/02791072.2013.847355

Domes, Gregor et al., 'Oxytocin Promotes Facial Emotion Recognition and Amygdala Reactivity in Adults with Asperger Syndrome', *Neuropsychopharmacology* (2013) https://www.nature.com/articles/npp2013254

Emmons, Robert A., *Thanks! How practicing gratitude can make you happier.* (Houghton Mifflin Company, 2008) ISBN: 9780547085739

Fox, Glenn R. et al., 'Neural correlates of gratitude' *Frontiers in Psychology* (2015) https://doi.org/10.3389/fpsyg.2015.01491

Gallup, Andrew C. and Church, Allyson M., 'The effects of intranasal oxytocin on contagious yawning', *Neuroscience Letters* (2015): 13–16 https://www.sciencedirect.com/science/article/abs/pii/S0304394015301336

Grant, Adam and Gino, Francesca, 'A little thanks goes a long way: Explaining why gratitude expressions motivate prosocial behavior', *Journal of Personality and Social Psychology* (2010) https://doi.org/10.1037/a0017935

Grewen, Karen M. et al, 'Effects of partner support on resting oxytocin, cortisol, norepinephrine, and blood pressure before and after warm partner contact', *Psychosomatic Medicine* (2005): 531–538 https://journals.lww.com/psychosomaticmedicine/Abstract/2005/07000/Effects_of_Partner_Support_on_Resting_Oxytocin,.4.aspx

Experimental Biology, 'How walking benefits the brain: Researchers show that foot's impact helps control, increase the amount of blood sent to the brain', *ScienceDaily* (2017) www.sciencedaily.com/releases/2017/04/170424141340.htm

Klein, Laura, 'All You Need is Love, Gratitude, and Oxytocin', *Greater Good Magazine*, The Greater Good Science Center at the University of California, Berkeley (2014) https://greatergood.berkeley.edu/article/item/love_gratitude_oxytocin

Kok, Bethany E. et al., 'How Positive Emotions Build Physical Health: Perceived Positive Social Connections Account for the Upward Spiral Between Positive Emotions and Vagal Tone', *Psychological Science* (2013) https://journals.sagepub.com/doi/10.1177/0956797612470827

Koole, Sander L. et al., 'Embodied Terror Management: Interpersonal Touch Alleviates Existential Concerns Among Individuals With Low Self-Esteem', *Psychological Science* (2013) https://journals.sagepub.com/doi/10.1177/0956797613483478

Kosfeld, Michael et al., 'Oxytocin increases trust in humans' *nature* (2005): 673–676 https://www.nature.com/articles/nature03701

Lambert, Nathaniel M. et al., 'Benefits of expressing gratitude: expressing gratitude to a partner changes one's view of the relationship', *Psychological Science* (2010) https://doi.org/10.1177/0956797610364003

Langer, E. J. (2023). *The Mindful Body*. Ballantine Books

Lawson, Elizabeth A., 'The effects of oxytocin on eating behaviour and metabolism in humans', *nature reviews/endocrinology* (2017): 700–709 https://www.nature.com/articles/nrendo.2017.115

Le Dorze, Claire et al., 'Emotional remodelling with oxytocin durably rescues trauma-induced behavioral and neuro-morphological changes in rats: a promising treatment for PTSD', *Translational Psychiatry* (2020) https://www.nature.com/articles/s41398-020-0714-0

Light, Kathleen C. et al., 'More frequent partner hugs and higher oxytocin levels are linked to lower blood pressure and heart rate in premenopausal women', *Biological Psychology* (2005) https://www.ncbi.nlm.nih.gov/pubmed/15740822/

Love, T. M. 'Oxytocin, motivation and the role of dopamine', in Pharmacol Biochem Behav. 2014 Apr;119:49-60. doi: 10.1016/j.pbb.2013.06.011. Epub 2013 Jul 9. PMID: 23850525; PMCID: PMC 3877159.

Lyubomirsky, Sonja et al., 'Pursuing Happiness: The Architecture of Sustainable Change', *Review of General Psychology* (2005) https://journals.sagepub.com/doi/10.1037/1089-2680.9.2.111

Mills, Paul et al., 'The role of gratitude in spiritual well-being in asymptomatic heart failure patients', *Spirituality in Clinical Practice* (2015) https://psycnet.apa.org/doi/10.1037/scp0000050

Nagasawa, Miho et al., 'Oxytocin-gaze positive loop and the coevolution of human-dog bonds', *Science* (2015): 333–336 https://science.sciencemag.org/content/348/6232/333

Nelson, C. A., Fox, N. A., and Zeanah, C. H., *Romania's Abandoned Children: Deprivation, brain development, and the struggle for recovery* (Harvard University Press, 2014)

Payne Bennett, Mary and Lengacher, Cecile, 'Humor and Laughter May Influence Health. III: Laughter and Health Outcomes', *Evidence-based complementary and alternative medicine* (2008) https://www.ncbi.nlm.nih.gov/pmc/articles/PMC2249748/

Peltola, Mikko J. et al., 'Oxytocin promotes face-sensitive neural responses to infant and adult faces in mothers', *Psychoneuroendocrinology* (2018): 261–280 https://www.sciencedirect.com/science/article/pii/S0306453017311927

Popova, Maria, 'Leonard Bernstein on Cynicism, Instant Gratification, and Why Paying Attention Is a Countercultural Act of Courage and Resistance', *Brainpickings* https://www.brainpickings.org/2016/10/03/dinner-with-lenny-leonard-bernstein-jonathan-cott/

Purves, Dale et al., 'Physiological Changes Associated with Emotion' *Neuroscience*. Sinauer Associates (2001) https://www.ncbi.nlm.nih.gov/books/NBK10829/

Richards, Sabrina, 'Pleasant to the Touch', *The Scientist* (2012) https://www.the-scientist.com/features/pleasant-to-the-touch-40534

Shea, Molly, 'The 7 Types of Rest You Need to Actually Feel Recharged', Shine, 2019. https://advice.shinetext.com/articles/the-7-types-of-restyou-need-to-actually-feel-recharged/

Strean, William B., 'Laughter prescription', *Canadian family physician* (2009) https://www.ncbi.nlm.nih.gov/pmc/articles/PMC2762283/

Sundman, Ann-Sofie et al., 'Long-term stress levels are synchronized in dogs and their owners', *Scientific Reports* (2019) https://www.nature.com/articles/s41598-019-43851-x

'The Science of Gratitude. A white paper prepared for the John Templeton Foundation by the Greater Good Science Center at UC Berkeley', *Greater Good Science Center* (2018) https://ggsc.berkeley.edu/images/uploads/GGSC-JTF_White_Paper- Gratitude-FINAL.pdf

Tjew A Sin, Mandy and Koole, Sander L., 'That human touch that means so much: Exploring the tactile dimension of social life', *The Inquisitive Mind* (2013) https://www.in-mind.org/article/that-human-touch-that-means-so-much-exploring-the-tactile-dimension-of-social-life

Tolle, E., *The Power of Now: A guide to spiritual enlightenment* (New World Library, 1999)

Tronick, Edward, 'Still Face Experiment', *University of Massachusetts Boston*. YouTube, (2009) https://www.youtube.com/watch?v=vmE3NfB_HhE

Tuomi, Janne, 'The effects of Whole-Body Vibration therapy on patients with primary insomnia', *University of Helsinki* (2016) https://helda.helsinki.fi/handle/10138/159913

Uvnäs-Moberg, Kerstin et al., 'Self-soothing behaviors with particular reference to oxytocin release induced by non-noxious sensory stimulation', *Frontiers in Psychology* (2015) https://www.frontiersin.org/articles/10.3389/fpsyg.2014.01529/full

Uvnäs-Moberg, Kerstin and Petersson, Maria, 'Oxytocin, a mediator of anti-stress, well-being, social interaction, growth and healing', *Z Psychosom Med Psychother* (2005) https://pubmed.ncbi.nlm.nih.gov/15834840/

World Health Organization, 'WHO launches commission to foster social connection' (2023) https://www.who.int/news/item/15-11-2023-who-launches-commission-to-foster-social-connection

White, Mathew P. et al., 'Spending at least 120 minutes a week in nature is associated with good health and wellbeing', *Scientific Reports* (2019) https://rdcu.be/b3K5P

Wong, Joel and Brown, Joshua: 'How Gratitude Changes You and Your Brain', *Greater Good Magazine*, The Greater Good Science Center at the University of California, Berkeley (2017) https://greatergood.berkeley.edu/article/item/how_gratitude_changes_you_and_your_brain

Zahn, Roland et al., 'The Neural Basis of Human Social Values: Evidence from Functional MRI', *Cerebral Cortex* (2008): 276–283 https://doi.org/10.1093/cercor/bhn080

Zak, Paul J., 'The Neuroscience of Trust', *Harvard Business Review* (2017) https://hbr.org/2017/01/the-neuroscience-of-trust

Zak, Paul J., 'Trust, morality – and oxytocin?', *TEDGlobal* (2011) https://www.ted.com/talks/paul_zak_trust_morality_and_oxytocin

Uvnäs-Moberg, Kerstin and Petersson, Maria, 'Oxytocin, a mediator of anti-stress, well-being, social interaction, growth and healing', *Zeitschrift für Psychosomatische Medizin und Psychotherapie* (2015) https://www.vr-elibrary.de/doi/10.13109/zptm.2005.51.1.57

Acknowledgements

Writing this book has been a dream come true. My previous experiences of writing a book have been filled with intense highs and lows, and I've been on the edge of giving up multiple times. This process, however, has been blessed with an energy of joy and ease. This smoothness is a testament to the collective efforts of an amazing team.

I remember walking into the Albatros office in Stockholm and, from the moment I stepped in, I felt at home. After our first meeting, I walked out elevated. I finally felt that these people saw me and understood my vision. We all felt confident that, together, we could make it happen. After only a few months, we found the perfect home for this book with Penguin Random House UK. So, thank you to my hard working agent William Crona, Martina Österling, Moa Alfvén and the rest of the Albatros team.

I also want to express a special thank you to Linda Helistö, one of the key players on this project. Your unique contributions and insights have been invaluable. We have a very special co-creation energy, and it was a true blessing to have you by my side throughout the process. As a team player, I felt you would catch every idea I threw out, even the less polished ones, and throw it back with more magic.

Thank you to Anya Hayes, Senior Editor at Penguin Random House, for asking the right questions and for all your help ensuring the end result is easily understandable and applicable. And thank you to my amazing editor, Julia Kellaway, for elevating the text to new heights. Your vast experience, combined with a deeper understanding, was priceless. Thank you also Laura Marchant, for excellent work with the copy-editing. Also a heartfelt thank you to Harriet Dundea from Carver PR for magically popping into this journey to help this book find its way to readers.

I want also to thank my amazing and wise friends who keep lifting me up – you know who you are. Special thanks to Miina Lange and Helen Hillersröm Miksche for helping the doors to open and this book to come alive.

I want to thank my love, Ukko, for being my safe haven – something I had actually written on my dream map a few years ago. You give me not only unconditional love but also the space to shine, which I finally have learned to receive.

An infinite thanks go to my family for giving me strong roots and wings to fly and Mammi for making me believe I could do whatever I want in this life.

And, finally, thank you to all the researchers, teachers and thought leaders that have crossed my path and are changing the world for the better with their work.

And to life, for all the twists and turns, and for helping me come back to myself with a bag full of purpose.